. . . a video cassette is jammed in your VCR?
. . . a cabinet door won't stay closed?
. . . the water in the toilet keeps running?
. . . the refrigerator makes loud noises?
. . . you need to replace a light switch?
. . . the stereo speakers sound distorted?
. . . your computer screen is blank?
. . . the furnace isn't heating properly?
. . . the oil in your car engine needs to be changed?
. . . the vacuum cleaner clogs up?

THE SIMPLE FIX-IT BOOK
will show you how to do the job—
and do it right!

THE
SIMPLE FIX-IT BOOK

MICHAEL O'BRIAN

BERKLEY BOOKS, NEW YORK

THE SIMPLE FIX-IT BOOK

A Berkley Book / published by arrangement with
Boldface Publishing

PRINTING HISTORY
Berkley edition / June 1993

ISBN: 0-425-13713-9

A BERKLEY BOOK ® TM 757,375
Berkley Books are published by The Berkley Publishing Group,
200 Madison Avenue, New York, New York 10016.
The name "BERKLEY" and the "B" logo
are trademarks belonging to Berkley Publishing Corporation.

PRINTED IN THE UNITED STATES OF AMERICA

10 9 8 7 6 5 4 3 2 1

Contents

Introduction

When something breaks in your house, you are at least annoyed, often inconvenienced, and sometimes faced with serious damage to other belongings. On top of that, you may also end up with an expensive repair bill. Learning how to fix things yourself can give you self-satisfaction, return immediate use of the damaged item, avoid further damages, and save you money.

Basic repairs, whether to the house itself or to the things in it, are often relatively simple and inexpensive. The two basic requirements for home repairs are knowledge and the proper tools. This book will give you the knowledge and tell you how to get the proper tools. With that knowledge, you will have the confidence to attempt and to complete many basic home repairs that you would never have thought of trying in the past.

There are no deep dark secrets to fixing most common things around the house. It is simply a matter of determining what is wrong and correcting it. Repairs are usually a simple matter of repairing or replacing a broken or nonfunctioning part. Everyone has heard dozens of stories about a plumber or electrician charging $50 to replace a 50-cent part. The reason is the cost of labor. When you learn to fix things yourself, you are paying yourself for your labor, and saving the most expensive part of most repair bills. You will have some up-front costs for tools that you don't have already. But think of these costs as the investments that they really are. Even buying some tools for a particular repair, you will still come out ahead of paying a professional. And you won't have to buy the tools the next time you need them. Also keep in mind that big, expensive, specialized tools can be rented for one-time use, and the people at the rental store will usually be able to give you complete directions on use. (If they can't, rent the tool someplace else.)

CHAPTER

1

. . . .

Tools and Hardware

Like many clichés, the old saying about the right tool for the job has a lot of truth in it. Trying to perform home repairs with the wrong tool will be difficult at best. At worst, it can cause even more damage, if not completely ruin what you are trying to fix. Even the simple matter of using the wrong-size screwdriver can result in much more extensive, and expensive, repairs than you started with.

Think of tools as a long-term investment. Don't try to get by without the right tool just because you don't have it in your toolbox. If you can't borrow it, go out and buy it. Even with the cost of the new tool, your total expense for the repair will probably be less than calling in a professional to do the repair. In addition, you will then have the tool, and it will be there the next time you need it for anything.

Always buy quality tools. The money you save in buying cheap tools is no savings. Using a poor-quality tool is just as bad as using the wrong tool. You may be able to get the job done, but often you can't. You may end up causing the same damage you would have done using the wrong tool, or the tool will bend or break in the middle of the job. Then you get mad and go out and buy the good tool you should have bought in the first place. Do it right the first time, and think of good tools as a lifetime investment.

In fact, many tools are guaranteed for life. Shop around,

especially if you are not used to buying tools. Ask about guarantees. You will find that even so simple a thing as a screwdriver or a pair of pliers may be guaranteed against defects and breakage. These guarantees are real, and are generally honored without question. Many national companies have their reputations based on their tool guarantees, and firmly stand behind them. The peace of mind from knowing that your money is well spent, and that you will probably never use the guarantee, is well worth the small additional amount you will pay for a top quality tool.

BASIC HAND TOOLS

Any household should have a basic collection of all-purpose hand tools. These would include screwdrivers, pliers, wrenches, and a hammer or two. Depending on the type of repairs you do, you will probably want to have several different handsaws. Screwdrivers come in two basic designs: flat-blade and Phillips. A flat-bladed screwdriver fits into the single slot in the head of a standard screw. The bigger the screw, the bigger the screwdriver you should be using. As the screw head gets bigger the slot is not only longer, but wider too. The tip of the screwdriver should fit as snugly as possible into the slot of the screw. But if the screwdriver is too big, it simply won't fit into the screw slot. But if the screwdriver is too small, it can slip and damage either the screwdriver or the screw. If you are trying to remove a screw with a wrong-size screwdriver and damage the screwhead, you may not be able to get the screw out. You are then faced with a tough and messy job of drilling out a screw.

Phillips screw slots are cross-shaped, and the tip of the Phillips screwdriver is pointed. The pointed, cross-shaped tip makes it much more difficult for the screwdriver to slip out of the screwhead slot while turning. Phillips screws are therefore used on finely finished surfaces to protect against damage from slipping screwdrivers. Here again, it is important to use the right-size screwdriver to avoid damage to the screwhead and to surrounding surfaces from a slipping screwdriver.

Screwdrivers should be used for turning screws, and not for other jobs. Don't use a screwdriver as a pry bar or a chisel or for any other job it is not designed for. It is very easy to damage the tip of a screwdriver when using it for some other purpose. And a damaged tip will damage screws or materials, making the screwdriver useless. A damaged or worn screwdriver tip can be ground back into shape if it is not damaged too badly. Use a power grinder if one is available to return the tip to a square shape. Otherwise put the screwdriver in a vise and restore the tip with a file. Screwdrivers are often sold in sets, and a good set will include all the sizes you will normally need. A good set of screwdrivers will usually include three or four flat-bladed screwdrivers and two or three Phillips screwdrivers.

Every home needs at least one hammer, and as you do more and more around the house, you will no doubt find it best to have several hammers. The basic hammer is a nail hammer, also known as a clawhammer because of the curved claw on the back of the head, used to pull nails. The clawhammer comes in different sizes, usually denoted by weight. The standard is a 16-ounce hammer. Professionals sometimes use a heavier 20-ounce hammer, and lighter ones are available, including 13-ounce and 7-ounce models. A variation on the clawhammer is the ripping hammer. This is similar in appearance, but the claw is much flatter. The claw on this hammer is designed to be worked in between pieces of wood to pry them apart.

Other hammers include the tack hammer and the ball

peen. The tack hammer is light and has a very small head. The head is often magnetized to hold tacks so that they can be tapped into the wood to start them. A ball-peen hammer is used for heavy pounding and to shape metal. You may also want to get a rubber mallet for pounding on softer items and to use with chisels.

Pliers are a very useful all-around tool, but they are also one of the most misused. Pliers are used for grabbing, bending, and even cutting. But they should not be used in place of a wrench. Wrenches are used to turn nuts and bolts. Using pliers on nuts or bolts will often result in damage to the fastener, rounding the corners and making it difficult if not impossible to turn. Variations on pliers include electrician's pliers, needle-nose pliers, locking pliers, and channel-lock pliers. Electrician or lineman's pliers are used to cut, strip, and bend wire. Needle-nose pliers are useful for small objects or working in tight spaces. Locking pliers clamp down firmly on a variety of objects, and can be used to turn damaged nuts or bolts that will no longer accept a wrench. Channel-lock, or multiple-joint pliers adjust to a wide size range and can be used to hold or turn jar lids, pipes, hose fittings, and many other things found around the home.

At a minimum, you should have a couple of different-size adjustable wrenches. These are generally referred to as crescent wrenches (the name was originally a trademark of the Crescent Tool Co.). An adjustable wrench is much better than a pair of pliers, but not as good as using the proper-size wrench.

The best wrench is a socket wrench or a box-end wrench. Because of the way they're constructed, these wrenches put pressure on several surfaces of the nut and bolt, spreading out the force and minimizing damage. A good set of socket wrenches is hard to beat for versatility. With extensions and adaptors, a socket set can handle a wide range of jobs properly. If you don't have a socket set or set of box wrenches, or can't use them because of space limitations, the next best thing is an open-end wrench. These wrenches only apply pressure to the fastener on two surfaces, but they are properly sized for the nut or bolt. Never try to use a metric wrench on a standard fastener, or vice versa. Damage is almost a certainty.

No home tool kit is complete without a couple of handsaws, including a hacksaw. The hacksaw is used to cut metal. It has interchangeable blades that can be replaced when worn, and changed to fit the material. Heavier metal calls for a coarser blade, while thin metal requires a finer blade. Hacksaws are designed to cut on the downstroke, so make sure that replacement blades are mounted properly.

The most common wood saw is the crosscut saw. This is a fairly long saw, usually 20 inches or more in length. The crosscut saw is used to cut wood across the grain. These saws are available in a range from coarse to fine, with the coarseness measured in teeth (or points) per inch. A useful all-around crosscut saw is a 10-point saw. Ripsaws are used to cut lumber along the grain. A 5½-point saw is a good all-purpose saw. The crosscut saw should be held at about a 45-degree angle to the wood while cutting, while the ripsaw works better at a flatter angle. When using a ripsaw to make a long cut, have some small pieces of scrap wood handy. As the cut gets longer and longer, put a scrap of wood in the cut to keep the board from binding the saw blade.

Other hand saws include the coping saw for cutting curves, and the box saw, used for cutting precise angles. The box saw is usually used in conjunction with a miter box to cut angles on wood or trim that will be joined together.

Most kinds of saws are usually available with either

plastic or wood handles. Plastic handles usually are more durable, but wood handles are more comfortable, particularly when you are working for longer periods of time.

OTHER HAND TOOLS

In addition to the basic tools, you will find a number of accessories to be very helpful. A ruler of some kind is absolutely necessary for home projects, and the handiest type is a tape measure with a belt clip. Various kinds of clamps, both screw type and spring type, are used to hold things down while you work on them or hold things together while you glue or screw or nail them together. A square is handy for marking straight lines, and a level helps keep things straight. A combination square is a small square with an adjustable leg that also includes a small level. It is probably the best buy for a starter tool kit. As you gain experience and expertise, you will add other, more specialized hand tools, such as hex-key wrenches, chisels, files, rasps, and planes.

Files and rasps are used for smoothing and shaping metal and wood. Files are used on metal and rasps are used on wood. Files are also used to sharpen other tools. Files may be flat or shaped and tapered. The latter are usually triangular or round, and are used for smoothing small areas, for detail work, or for working inside a hole or an odd opening.

Files and rasps have a smooth, tapered, pointed end called the tang. You can either hold the tool by the tang or you can put a plastic or wooden handle over the tang for a better (and less painful) grip. The file does its cutting on the downstroke, as you push on the tang. For heavy work, push on the tang with one hand while pressing down on the other end of the file with the free hand. Clean built-up material out of the file teeth with a wire brush.

Files and rasps come in a wide range of coarseness. Two or three different-grade files will cover the range of most work you will encounter. To remove a lot of material with a file, start with a coarse file and change to a finer one as you near your goal. Some wood rasps are available with one coarse side and one fine side. This should cover most home-fix-it situations.

Files do get dull with use. Unlike most other hand tools, they cannot be sharpened. Dull files have to be discarded and replaced.

Wood can also be shaped with planes and chisels. A plane is a hand tool that holds a sharp blade that is pushed across wood to remove smooth, thin shavings. Planes come in different shapes and sizes, larger ones being more useful for removing large amounts of wood, while smaller ones are best for detailed work. Planes are used to smooth and shape wood. Hold the plane firmly and maintain forward pressure without rocking the tool. Apply downward pressure at the same time that you push forward. Hold the plane at a slight angle to the direction in which you are pushing. Keep the blade set at a fairly thin depth, and make several passes to remove a given thickness of wood rather than trying to remove it all in one pass. Plane handles work loose with use, so make sure that you keep the handle tight.

Chisels are used to cut into wood and remove specific shapes or pieces, such as fitting a hinge into a door. A chisel is simply a long piece of metal with a sharp blade at one end and a handle at the other end. The handle end is designed to be tapped with a hammer or mallet, or to be struck lightly or pushed with the free hand for fine detailed work. Chisels are measured across the blade, usually in quarter-inch increments. A typical set would have four chisels, measuring ¼, ½, ¾, and 1 inch.

Do not use chisels for any purpose other than cutting wood. Don't try to remove all the wood with a few heavy mallet blows on the chisel. Rather, chip away at the wood, using light taps and taking small slivers. If removing a lot of wood, you can make rough cuts at the start, and make finer and finer cuts as you near the end. Finish up with very light taps. Even better, put down the hammer and use the heel of your free hand to strike the chisel.

Keep chisels and all cutting tools sharp. The best method is to use a power grinder to put a sharp edge on the tool and then use a sharpening stone for the final edge. Set the tool rest on the grinder for about a 25-degree edge on the tool. Move the edge back and forth across the grinder, taking care not to let the tool get too hot. You don't need to press hard on the tool. After you have a good edge on the tool, finish it with an aluminum-oxide sharpening stone. Lay the blade flat on the stone and stroke it lightly in the direction of the sharp edge. Lift the blade off the stone on the backstroke. After four or five strokes, turn the tool over and repeat on the other side.

Clamps are very useful for holding down the material that you are working on, for holding together two pieces that are to be drilled or joined, or for holding together glued pieces until the glue dries. The common C-clamp is handy for small jobs and is available in many sizes, but it is shallow and can't hold larger pieces. Hand screws are more versatile. They have large wooden jaws that are tightened by a pair of long parallel bolts that join the two jaws and are screwed in from opposite directions. The jaws of the hand screws do not have to be kept parallel, and can thus apply constant pressure on objects that are not square. Bar clamps are sets of movable jaws mounted on a bar or pipe, often many feet long. They are very useful in furniture repair. Spring clamps can be applied and removed easily with one hand, either to hold two pieces together or to hold the material you are working on to a table or workbench.

SUPPLIES

As you do more and more home-fix-it jobs, you will begin to amass a good-size collection of materials such as glue, sandpaper, and so on. If possible, try to get some of the basics before you need them, so you won't find yourself driving to the hardware store for a sheet of sandpaper in the middle of a project.

A good all-purpose white glue, available from any grocery or drugstore, will serve most purposes, from gluing a photo in an album to gluing a leg back on a chair. (The chair leg, unlike the photo, will need to be held firmly in place until the glue is completely dried). Carpenters' glue is better for bigger, heavy-duty projects involving large pieces of wood. Contact cement is used for gluing large surfaces together, but is not appropriate for gluing edges.

So-called super glue is useful for many mending jobs, particularly when fixing delicate things. Epoxy cement is a two-part adhesive. The two materials are mixed together at the time of use. This is generally the strongest adhesive you can use, and some types dry very quickly, although there is usually a trade-off between drying time and strength.

Caulk is available in tubes or cans, and is used to seal joints and make them waterproof. Glazing compound is a modern replacement for window putty. The compound will hold and seal the windowpane, but will not turn hard and brittle as putty will.

Rubber cement is used to glue flexible materials together, or to glue a flexible material to a rigid one. Silicone-rubber cement is a waterproof sealer that comes in tubes or cans and is used to caulk bathtubs and for other purposes.

In addition to various paints that you accumulate over time, you will also need a general paint thinner, such as mineral spirits, and perhaps turpentine and a lacquer thinner for cleaning brushes. While stains can be put on with a brushlike disposable sponge, you should have good brushes or a good roller for painting. A well-built paint roller will last forever. Just slip on new cylinders as the old ones wear out. You can also purchase cheap, disposable plaster liners for roller trays to eliminate that messy cleanup job.

One or two good putty knives are also handy for applying putty and Spackle. The blade should be firm but flexible. A scraper with replaceable razor blades works best for removing paint splatters, labels, etc., from glass and other hard surfaces.

A well-equipped workbench should have several grades of sandpaper. The grit or coarseness of sandpaper is stated numerically. The higher the number, the finer the sandpaper. For general purposes, 50-, 100-, and 200-grit sandpaper should take care of most jobs. A small, inexpensive holder makes sandpaper much easier to use.

You will also need some kind of lubricant for various uses. The handiest all-purpose lubricant is a light machine oil in a spray can. There are various brand names, and most hardware or discount department stores carry a house brand or generic brand. Use it to lubricate moving parts, to clean parts, and to loosen stuck nuts and bolts.

Eventually, you will want a good-size tool box to hold everything. The next step is a workbench in the garage or basement, often with a Peg-Board mounted over it to hold tools, and a vise to hold lumber or other objects. A workbench is a good do-it-yourself project, easily made with a frame of 2x4s and some 1x8s for the top. The result will be cheaper and sturdier than anything available in stores for a reasonable price.

POWER TOOLS

More and more people are buying power tools for use around the house. If there is one power tool in a home, it is probably an electric drill. Few people have or use hand drills anymore, and many youngsters may have never seen a hand drill.

Electric drills are simple and straightforward, varying only in features and size. Drills designed for home use have their size stated in terms of the largest diameter bit they will hold, usually ¼, ⅜, or ½ inch. A ⅜-inch drill is generally adequate for most home uses. The common features are variable speed and reversibility. A variable-speed drill turns the bit faster as the trigger is pulled back. This is very useful for starting holes at very slow speeds. Reversibility is not needed if all you are going to do is drill holes, but it is necessary if you are going to use the drill for other purposes, such as using a screwdriver attachment on it. The variable-speed feature is also needed for these applications.

After the electric drill, the next power-tool addition to the home workshop is usually a power saw. The two basic types are the saber saw and the circular saw. The saber saw, sometimes called a portable jigsaw, has a small knifelike blade that projects down from the bottom of the saw and moves up and down very rapidly. The saber saw can cut most materials, and can be used to cut curves and angles. A wide variety of blades is available, ranging from fine to coarse, and designed for wood, plywood, and metals. Remember that a saber saw cuts on the upstroke, so the side of the material that you want to end up with the best finish should be facing down when cutting.

A circular saw is used for rougher cuts on lumber. It is a heavy saw and requires some practice in order to make precise cuts. It is generally used for dimension lumber, 2x4 or larger in size.

Electric sanders come in a variety of sizes and styles. Belt sanders rotate a belt of sandpaper in a straight-line motion, while orbital sanders move in a circular pattern. Depending on the material, the swirls left by orbital sanders can be difficult to eliminate with hand sanding.

A router is a cutting tool used to cut grooves or dovetails, to bevel, or to round corners or edges. There are many different router bits available, making a limitless variety of effects possible. Good results with a router require lots of practice.

Larger power tools are more for the hobby category than for home fix-it. These tools can include such things as a drill press, a table saw, or even a lathe. Tools like this are used to make furniture and other wood objects rather than to repair things.

HARDWARE

The primary hardware for home repairs consists of nails and screws. Nails are often the easiest method for completing a quick repair, but screws are preferable. It is important to be very careful when nailing that you don't split the wood, particularly when working on small objects. The safest method is to drill a hole in the wood before nailing. When nailing lumber, avoid putting the nails in a straight line along the grain, or the wood could split. Nails hold better if driven in at an angle, rather than perpendicular to the surface. When joining large pieces of lumber, such as when constructing your home workbench, apply carpenter's glue on the facing surfaces before nailing.

Nails come in a wide variety of sizes and styles. Make sure that the nails you use are right for the job. A few of the many types of nails available include common nails; finishing nails, which have very small heads; flooring nails, which have a screwlike twist; and double-headed form nails, which are designed to be removed after temporary use. Pick a nail size such that the point will not come close to going through the material that you are nailing to. Use a special tool called a nail set to finish driving a nail below the surface of wood.

Nails are traditionally stated in a size known as the penny, abbreviated ''d.'' A six-penny, or 6d, nail is 2 inches long, while a twenty-penny, or 20d, nail is 4 inches long. Nails smaller than 4d (1½ inches long) are called brads and are measured in inches. Nails bigger than 20d are called spikes, and are also measured in inches.

Screws come with slotted heads or Phillips heads. Phillips-head screws are best for finish work, as the screwdriver is less likely to slip and damage the material. Flat-head screws are designed to be countersunk (driven in with the screw head flush with the surface), while pan-head screws remain protruding above the material. To drive flat-head screws in properly, you will need a countersink, a small boring device that works with an electric drill. Drill the holes for the screw, and then use the countersink to bevel around the hole just big enough for the screw head.

Always drill a pilot hole before using a screw. Use a drill bit slightly smaller than the screw shank, which is the solid core inside the screw threads. Use a center punch on metal to make a small dent before drilling. This will prevent the drill from slipping and scratching the surface. When drilling metal, it is best to use a variable-speed drill and to use a very low speed. This enables you to drill smoothly and to avoid burning up the drill bit.

Wood screws have threads running about two-thirds of the way up the shank from the point, while the rest of the shank up to the head is smooth. Metal screws (sometimes called sheet-metal screws) are self-tapping, meaning that it is only necessary to drill a hole in the metal, not to cut threads in the piece of metal to receive the screw. Metal screws have thread for the entire length of the screw.

Lag screws are very large wood screws that have hex heads, designed to be turned with a wrench rather than with a screwdriver. They are used for heavy lumber and timbers. They are similar to lag bolts, except that the lag screw is designed to screw into wood while the lag bolt is threaded into a nut.

Bolts are threaded fasteners designed to fit tightly into a predrilled hole and to be fastened with a nut on the other side of the materials being joined. Carriage bolts have threads about halfway up from the bottom, with a squared shank below the head to keep the bolt from turning when the nut is tightened. Machine bolts have either hexagonal or square heads that are held with a wrench while the nut is tightened. Stovebolts have slotted heads like screws. The head is held with a screwdriver while the nut is tightened with a wrench.

Rivets are metal fasteners that are usually beyond the needs and equipment of the do-it-yourselfer. An exception is the pop rivet. Pop rivets are easy to use and have the added advantage that access to the back of the material being riveted is not required. To use a pop rivet, simply drill a hole through the materials to be joined and insert a pop rivet. Place the pop-rivet tool over the rivet and squeeze the handle several times. The tool will pull the stem of the pop rivet, flaring the rivet on the back of the material.

A staple gun drives heavy-duty staples into wood and is very handy for working with plastic sheeting, screening, roofing, and other materials. Most good staple guns have adjustable pressure and will accommodate various-size staples. Light stapling jobs can be done with an office stapler that swings open.

Mending plates, brackets, and angle irons are useful for joining various materials together. A mending plate may be a simple length of metal with predrilled holes, or something more complex, such as an L-shaped or T-shaped plate. Brackets or angle irons can be used to join boards or metal at a right angle.

2

· · · · · · · · · · · ·

Plumbing

Plumbing repairs in the home usually boil down to one of two basic problems: leaks or clogged drains. Most of the simpler varieties of these problems can be fixed fairly easily, often with a few common tools and no special materials. Specialized plumbing tools include a plunger, an auger, and pipe wrenches. Before working on plumbing fixtures, the first step is always to shut off the water. Shutoff valves are usually easy to locate and to use. The valve is usually behind the toilet or under the sink. The handle is generally kept in either the fully on or the fully off position. After turning off the water, double-check by turning on a faucet or flushing the toilet. There is also a main shutoff valve in each house, usually located where the main waterline enters the house, in the basement or in a crawl space under the house. As a safety precaution, know where your main water valve is so that you can quickly get to it and shut off the water in case of a broken pipe.

CLOGGED DRAINS

One of the most common household plumbing problems is the clogged drain. It seems to happen most often with the toilet, followed by the kitchen sink. Clogs usually occur in the trap, a feature of the plumbing designed to prevent odors from backing up through the drainpipes from the sewer. The trap under a sink is a U-shaped pipe that is below the level of the drainpipe as it goes out through the wall. Water remains in the bottom of the U-shaped pipe sealing it off so that sewer gases cannot come up into the house. There is a tanklike trap built into the bottom of the toilet bowl.

The first line of attack on a clogged drain is the plunger, also known as the plumber's helper. Before working on a clogged drain, check to make sure that other drains in the house are working. If they aren't, you have a major blockage in the main drainpipes.

For a clogged toilet, the first step is to bail as much water as possible out of the bowl and then, wearing a rubber glove, to check the outlet in the bowl for obstructions. If there are none, make sure that there is enough water in the toilet bowl to cover the rubber bulb of the plunger. Put the plunger over the outlet in the toilet bowl and press down slowly and pull up quickly. This action is designed to pull the obstruction back up, rather than to force it further down into the pipe. Repeat for as long as several minutes if necessary. With a simple clog, the water should begin to flow out of the toilet bowl almost immediately. If the toilet is not unclogged after several minutes, the plunger is probably not going to work.

The next step for a clogged toilet is an auger, if you have one or can borrow or rent one. To use an auger, bail as much water as you can out of the toilet bowl. Then insert the curved end of the auger into the outlet opening and turn the handle to work the cable into the drain. When the cable hits the clog, try to pull it back out without turning the handle. If that doesn't work, try turning the handle of the auger back and forth to break up the clog. If the auger doesn't unclog the drain, you will have to call a plumber.

A clogged kitchen sink is usually caused by a buildup of

waste or garbage in the trap, the U-shaped or J-shaped pipe fitting directly under the sink. Clogs in the bathroom are usually caused by a buildup of hair and other material in the trap. It is sometimes possible to unclog a sink with a chemical drain cleaner or with a plunger. Follow the label directions for the chemical cleaner. If the sink has a built-in stopper, remove it before proceeding any further.

To use a plunger, first check to see if there is an overflow opening in the sink. If there is, plug it with a wet cloth. If you are working on a double sink, you will need to keep the drain in one side of the sink tightly covered or plugged with a damp cloth while applying pressure with the plunger on the other sink. Make sure that there is enough water in the sink to cover the rubber bulb of the plunger. Push the plunger down slowly and pull up quickly, maintaining a steady rhythm for several minutes if necessary.

If neither of these methods work, the next step is to check the trap. The trap is the U-shaped or J-shaped piece of pipe under the sink that connects the vertical drain from the sink to the horizontal pipe that leads into the wall. Start by removing most if not all the things that you have stored under the sink, particularly anything that could be damaged by water. Put a bucket under the trap. If the trap has a clean-out opening at the bottom, remove the clean-out plug with a wrench and let the trapped water flow into the bucket. Replace the plug and see if the sink is unclogged. If there is no plug, or if the drain is still clogged, remove the entire trap by loosening the fitting at each end of the pipe. You may need a pipe wrench to remove the collar at each end of the trap, but a channel lock will usually be sufficient. Plastic piping may even have flanges that can be turned by hand, requiring no tools. Be careful, because as you start to remove the trap, water and clogged material can rush out of the pipe. The clog will usually be caused by material trapped in the bottom of the curve. Remove any trapped material and replace the trap.

If there was nothing in the trap, or if the drain is still clogged, the clog is going to be further along the drainpipe. You will need an auger to clean out the pipe. Work the cable into the drainpipe by turning the handle, taking care not to ram it too hard, or you could loosen fittings or break old pipes inside the wall. If the sink is still clogged, you will need to call a plumber.

TOILET REPAIRS

Toilet repairs are usually fairly simple in concept, but are often difficult to do because of cramped quarters and inaccessible parts.

The toilet seat and the lid are usually a single unit that cannot be taken apart. The seat unit is fastened to the toilet bowl with two bolts on the back of the seat that fit through the back of the bowl and are fastened from the bottom with nuts. A loose seat can be tightened simply by tightening the nuts with a wrench. You may have to lie on the floor in a fairly tight space to accomplish this. Anything more serious than this generally calls for replacing the seat. Toilet seats are fairly standard in size, although they come in a wide range of colors and materials.

Most toilets are two-piece units, with a tank that sits on top of a bowl. The tank is fastened to the bowl with two long bolts that pass through the tank and through two holes in the back of the bowl, and are fastened with nuts under the bowl. There is a large waterproof gasket sealing the hole that allows water to flow from the tank to the bowl. The bowl is then bolted to the floor flange of the drainpipe, with a wax ring to seal the drain.

Running Water: A common problem with toilets is that

the water continues to run after the toilet is flushed. This is caused either by the stopper or flush ball in the bottom of the tank not closing properly, or by the float not turning off the water supply.

When you flush the toilet by pushing down on the flushing lever, you push up on an arm that is connected, usually by a chain, to a rubber stopper at the bottom of the tank. This allows the water in the tank to flow into the bowl, flushing the contents of the bowl down the drain and refilling the bowl with fresh water. When the water in the tank drains out, another arm with a bulblike float on the end goes down, opening a valve that refills the tank.

If the flush ball does not properly reseat itself in the opening in the bottom of the tank, water will run out of the tank and into the bowl. The ball will not seat properly if it is worn or if it is hung up on some other parts in the tank. Check to see that the flush ball can move freely and that it is down as far as it can go. If the flush ball is fully down and water is still running through the bottom of the tank, the ball is probably worn and needs to be replaced.

The other reason for the water to continue to run is that the float arm is not turning off the water. If this is the case, water will be running over the top of the vertical drainpipe that rises from the bottom of the tank. Lift the float arm. If this stops the running water, this is the cause of the problem, and the arm needs to be adjusted. If there is an adjustment screw on the valve end of the arm, turn it to lower the arm. If there is no adjustment, bend the arm down to lower the float. If this doesn't stop the running water, you will need to check the valve to see that nothing is hung up, and that the valve is working properly. If necessary, take the valve apart and replace the washer.

Toilet Won't Flush: If the toilet won't flush, or if you have to hold down the handle until it has completely flushed, there is some kind of problem in the linkage between the handle and the flush ball. First, lift the lid off the tank and check to see that the handle is tight. If it is not, tighten the nut on the inside of the tank. Then check to see that the refill tube that runs from the valve to the overflow drainpipe is not kinked. Next, push down on the handle and watch the resulting actions. Pushing down on the handle should lift the lever that is connected to the handle on the inside of the tank. The other end of the lever is connected, usually by wire or chain, to the flush ball. If the lever is raised but the flush ball does not come up, check to see that the connection between the lever and the flush ball has not come apart, that there is not too much slack in the connection, and that nothing is binding or getting hung up in the process. If the problem is caused by a broken connection, you may need to replace a chain or other broken part. Remove the part and take it to your local hardware store for a replacement part. Make sure that you get parts specifically designed for plumbing. Similar metal parts will work for a while, but can eventually corrode from being underwater all the time, and you will have to replace them again fairly soon.

Removing the Tank: Occasionally, you may have to remove the tank from the toilet, for better access for repairs, to paint or wallpaper behind the toilet, or for some other reason. The job is fairly straightforward, but it can be difficult. The first step is to turn off the water to the tank. This is done via a small valve on the pipe that comes out of the wall behind the toilet. Next, flush the toilet and check to see that the tank does not refill. Bail out any water remaining in the bottom of the tank if possible.

Place an empty bucket under the back of the tank, and put some old towels around the base of the toilet, particularly if the bathroom is carpeted. Use a wrench or a pair of channel-lock pliers to loosen and remove the tubing that runs from the wall valve to the bottom of the tank. Next, loosen and remove the two nuts on the underside of the back of the toilet bowl that hold down the tank. Lift the tank straight up off the bowl, immediately tilting it to one side to keep any remaining water from running out the center hole.

To replace the tank, simply reverse the steps listed above. The gasket that seals the joint between the tank and the bowl does not have to be replaced unless you have had a problem with water leaking around that joint.

DRIPPING FAUCETS

Dripping faucets are caused by worn seals or washers. If you know the make and model of the faucet you have, you can buy a kit from a hardware store or plumbing-supply house. If you don't, you will have to take the faucet apart and take the necessary parts to the store to get the replacements needed.

Older faucets are compression or stem-and-seal types. These have separate handles for the hot and cold water. Faucets using a single handle to control flow and temperature mix are either ball-type or cartridge faucets. Cartridge faucets may be disk-type or sleeve-type.

Compression Faucets: Before working on any faucet, turn off the water under the sink. For compression faucets, first remove the screws holding down the handles and remove the handles. (The screw may be under a pop-off index cap on top of the handle.) Use a wrench to remove the retaining nut and remove the stem (the core) from the faucet. The stem will have a washer on the bottom, held on with a screw, and an O-ring around the base near the bottom. Remove the washer with a screwdriver and remove the O-ring by cutting it off with a razor. Slide on a new

O-ring and replace the washer. Rub heat-proof grease on all parts of the stem and replace.

Ball-Type Faucets: A ball-type faucet has a single long handle that swivels up and down to change the water flow, and swivels left and right at the same time to change the temperature mix. Ball-type faucets can be moved diagonally to change both temperature and flow at the same time. You should purchase a repair kit for this type of faucet before beginning work.

There is a setscrew in the handle that should be loosened with a hex-key wrench or with the setscrew key included with the repair kit. Remove the handle, exposing the adjusting ring on top of the faucet. Tighten the adjusting ring with a pair of channel-lock pliers or with the adjusting wrench included in the repair kit. Put the handle back on and test for leaks. If the faucet still leaks, remove the handle again and unscrew the cap on top of the faucet with a pair of channel locks. Wrap a rag around the cap before removing to avoid scratches. Under the cap you will find a cam (a plastic ring), a round cam washer, and a rotating ball. Remove all of these parts. Under the rotating ball arc valve seats and springs, which should be removed with a screwdriver.

Next, remove the faucet spout by twisting upward. The remaining fixture will have two O-rings around it. These should be removed by cutting them off with a razor. Coat new O-rings with heat-proof grease and slide them into place. Slide the spout back on, pressing down until it rests on the plastic ring at the bottom of the fixture. Reinstall the new springs and valve seats included in the repair kit, followed by the new rotating ball, cam washer, and cam. Replace the cap and the handle.

Cartridge Faucets: Cartridge faucets also have a single handle to control the flow and the temperature. The handle on these faucets slides straight up and down to control the flow of the water, and it turns clockwise or counterclockwise to change the temperature. Disk-type cartridge faucets have a knob-type handle resembling the handles on compression faucets, while sleeve-type cartridge faucets have a long lever handle resembling the handle of a ball-type faucet. The difference here is that the lever moves up and down to control the flow, while the collar rotates to control the temperature.

To fix a disk-type faucet, turn off the water and pry off the index cap on top of the handle. Loosen the screw under the cap and remove the handle. Under the handle is a metal block, the handle inset, which is held in place by a setscrew. Loosen the setscrew with a hex-key wrench and remove the handle inset. Beneath that is the dome cap, which should be loosened and removed. Next remove the two mounting screws that hold the cartridge in place and remove the cartridge. Replace the cartridge with a new one and reassemble the faucet.

A sleeve-type cartridge faucet also has an index cap on top that should be pried off. Remove the handle screw under the cap, lift the lever to the highest position, and remove the handle. Next remove the large retaining nut with a pair of channel-lock pliers. Some faucets, particularly bathroom models, will have a grooved collar under the retaining nut that must also be removed. This will expose the cartridge, which will have a retaining clip holding it in place. Pull the retaining clip out using a pair of needle-nose pliers.

Grab the top of the cartridge with a pair of channel-lock pliers and pull straight up to remove. Twist the faucet spout and pull up to remove. Cut the old O-rings off the fixture with a razor. Spread heat-proof grease on the new O-rings and slide them on the fixture. Reassemble the faucet, installing a new cartridge.

WATER HEATERS

There are relatively few things that can go wrong with a water heater, and therefore there are not very many home repairs that can be done by the nonprofessional. If the water heater seems to be working but the water is not hot enough, there are two simple possible answers. The first is that your water heater is not large enough for your needs, and cannot keep up with demand. The only solution to this problem is to get a new, larger water heater. The second possibility is that the thermostat on your water heater is not set high enough. Check the setting and turn it up if necessary. But keep in mind that the higher the setting, the more energy you are going to use keeping the water hot around the clock for those times when you actually use it.

Water heaters have a safety valve on the top, which can trip and allow water to run out the top. This may occur because of an obstruction, which can be cleared by working the pumplike handle on the valve a few times. If the valve is defective, it will have to be replaced. To do this, turn off the water heater, unscrew the valve, and screw in a new one.

A total lack of hot water could occur from a tripped circuit breaker on an electric water heater, or a pilot-light flameout on a gas water heater. With an electric water heater, reset the circuit breaker and see if it trips again. If it does, there may be a wiring problem that should be fixed by a professional. With a gas water heater, if the pilot light cannot be relit following the instructions on the water heater, call a professional.

With these few exceptions, water heaters generally either work or they don't. And if they don't, they will have to be repaired or replaced by a professional.

LEAKING PIPES

Leaking pipes are usually serious problems that are beyond the abilities of the home handyman. If you do not have some specific plumbing experience, most leaks are best left to the experts. There are, however, some temporary fixes that may get you by until the plumber can get there.

The first thing to do when faced with a leaking pipe is to turn off the water, either at a fixture shutoff valve or at the main shutoff valve. Examine the area of the leak to see if you can pinpoint the leak. A leak at a fitting might be solved simply by tightening the joint. If a joint is leaking, it is best to disassemble the joint completely, clean the threads, apply pipe dope (a thread sealant), and reassemble the joint.

Temporary fixes to other leaks include applying epoxy cement to the leaking area, wrapping the leak with electrician's tape, and clamping a rubber patch or some kind of gasket material over the leak with a hose clamp, a C-clamp, or some other holding device.

CHAPTER
3

. . . .

Electrical Repairs

Electricity can be dangerous, but this should not stop you from attempting simple repairs on electrical circuits, fixtures, or appliances in your home. The first rule of working with electrical circuits or electrical equipment is to make sure that the circuit does not have power and that the equipment is not plugged in. Failure to follow that simple rule is the cause of the vast majority of problems and accidents in working with electricity.

Service Panel: Electricity enters the house through the service panel. In older houses, the service panel is a fuse box. Modern homes have all electrical circuits running from circuit breakers instead of fuses in the service panel. A circuit is a closed electrical system that may be as simple as a pair of wires going to a major appliance, or as complex as a system of outlets or lights and switches in various rooms of the house. Each circuit has a circuit breaker in the service panel. The service panel is located on the inside of the house, and is usually a rectangular, gray, metal box with a hinged cover that swings up from the bottom. Inside the box are switches or circuit breakers, usually arranged in two vertical columns. Each switch is a circuit breaker that controls the flow of electricity to all outlets or electrical connections on that particular circuit or wiring loop.

If there is a short or an overload on a particular circuit, the circuit breaker trips, shutting off the flow of electricity to that circuit. Throwing the switch back to its original position will restore electricity to the circuit. This should be done only after reducing the electrical load on the circuit or checking for a short circuit, otherwise the circuit breaker will continue to trip. If a circuit breaker continues to trip even with a light load, there may be a short in a wire or an appliance. Unplug any appliances you have on that circuit and inspect each for possible defects.

Fuses: Fuses provide the same safety factor as modern circuits, but fuses cannot be reset or reused. When a fuse blows because of a short or an overload, it must be replaced with a new fuse. Fuses are rated according to the capacity of the circuit that they are protecting. Do not replace a blown fuse with a higher-rated fuse. That will allow more power to flow to the circuit than it is designed to handle, leading to possible damage or even a fire. And never attempt to circumvent a fuse. The fuse is there to protect against damage and fire. Attempting to defeat the purpose of the fuse greatly increases the probability of burning down the house.

Circuits and Loads: If the circuit breakers have not been labeled as to which areas of the house or which major appliances are on each circuit, you should begin to keep track of this information as you work with the electricity in your home. Each circuit breaker in the service panel should be labeled as to its capacity. This capacity is stated in amperes or amps. Most residential circuit breakers are 15 or 20 amps. Circuits are generally designed for a maximum load of about 1500 watts. This would be the equivalent of about 15 100-watt bulbs. You would not want to run a full load on a circuit, but should keep the load well under the maximum.

Lamps, radios, clocks, sewing machines, and other small

appliances generally use less than 100 watts each. Larger appliances such as three-way lamps, hair dryers, or window fans may use electricity in the 150-to-300-watt range. A television or a coffee maker could be in the 400-to-700-watt range. High-heat appliances such as an iron or a waffle maker can use as much as 1000 watts.

Safety: If you flip a switch in the service panel to the off position, no electricity will flow through that particular circuit, and there will be no electrical power in any outlet or fixture wired to that circuit. When working on a wire or switch or fixture, make sure that the circuit breaker is off before starting. When in doubt, turn the master switch to the off position to turn off the power to the entire house.

If you do any work on electrical circuits or fixtures, it is a good idea to buy a voltage tester. This inexpensive device will tell you if electricity is connected to the outlet or switch or fixture you are working on. The tester is a small neon bulb with two wires ending in metal prongs. To test an outlet for electricity, simply insert the prongs into the rectangular slots. If there is power, the bulb will glow.

The voltage tester can also be used to test an outlet for proper grounding. Insert one probe into the ground slot (the round or arched hole under the two rectangular slots) and the other probe into the smaller of the two rectangular slots. If the outlet is properly grounded, the bulb will glow. (If you have older outlets with both rectangular slots the same size, you may need to try the second probe in both slots to get the bulb to glow.) You can also test the cover-plate ground by placing one probe on the cover-plate screw and inserting the other in the small rectangular slot. The bulb will glow if the plate is properly grounded.

When working on an outlet, check the electricity again after removing the cover plate. Touch one probe to the brass-colored screw on one side of the outlet, and the other probe to the silver-colored screw directly opposite. If the bulb glows, return to the service panels and turn off the electricity. For a switch, simply touch the probes to the two screws holding the wires to the switch. For a wall or ceiling fixture, lower the fixture enough to expose the wiring connections and touch the tester probes to the screws that connect the wires to the fixture.

Never work on any electrical appliance that is plugged into an outlet. If you are working on something and must plug it in to test it, make sure that all wiring connections are properly covered and protected before inserting the plug. And make sure that you pull the plug again before resuming work.

As a double precaution, make sure that your tools are insulated and that you are not grounded when working with electrical equipment or circuits. Proper tools for working with electricity have rubber or plastic handles. Don't work on electrical circuits while standing on bare ground or on concrete, when barefoot, or when your feet or the surface upon which you are standing are wet. As an added precaution, wear rubber-soled shoes when working with electricity.

Extension Cords: Extension cords are a routine part of electrical usage in most homes. Some appliances may be used exclusively with an extension cord, such as a lamp that is located too far from any outlet. Portable power tools are often used with extension cords to reach various locations at once, or to avoid the problem of having to move the objects being repaired closer to an outlet. Properly used, extension cords are a useful tool. Improperly used, they can be dangerous.

The length of the cord causes the voltage to drop as it travels along the extension cord. The longer cord and the thinner the wire, the more voltage is lost. A 10-percent drop in voltage can reduce an electric motor's power by 20 percent. Severe voltage drop can weaken a motor enough to burn it out. The resistance of a thin cord also results in heating of the wire. An extension cord can heat up enough to damage the cord and even start a fire.

Using a thicker cord both lessens heating of the wire and decreases voltage drop. Always use a cord that is heavy enough to supply the power needed by the appliance or tool. Most heavy appliances and power tools have the required amperage stated on the nameplate. If the power usage is stated in watts, divide that number by 120 to obtain the amps (amps equal watts divided by voltage, and voltage is 120 in this country).

If the power consumption in amps is under seven, use a 16-gauge extension cord for up to 50 feet, and a 14-gauge for up to 100 feet. For power consumption in the 8-to-14-amp range, use a 16-gauge cord up to 25 feet, a 14-gauge cord for 25 to 50 feet, and a 12-gauge cord for up to 100 feet. For 15 to 18 amps, use a 14-gauge extension cord for distances up to 25 feet, a 12-gauge cord for 25 to 50 feet, and a 10-gauge cord for up to 100 feet.

WIRING

Electrical wiring is standard throughout the country. Electricians must follow their local code in installing and repairing wiring, and these codes are very similar from one part of the country to another. Electricity is carried over a pair of wires or conductors, one of which is the "hot" side or wire, and other of which is the "ground" side. The wires are always enclosed in some kind of protective casing or insulation. Generally, the insulation on the individual wires is colored, with black or red insulation denoting the hot side and white insulation denoting the ground. Circuits with a special ground circuit use a third wire for the ground, which is usually covered in green insulation.

Outlets: A standard electrical outlet has places to plug in two appliances, and is covered with a rectangular plate held in place by a single small screw. If you remove the plate, turning off the power to that outlet first, you will see that the outlet is mounted with two small screws to the front of a box. The metal box is large enough to hold the outlet and the wires connected to it. There are usually two wires, one white and one black, coming into the box through a small hole, and two similar wires going back out of the box.

The wires are fastened to the outlet body, with the white wires on one side of the outlet and the black wires on the opposite side. The white wires should always be fastened with silver screws and the black wires with brass screws. (What is important here is the color of the screws, not the materials that they are made from.) If there are only two wires coming into the box and none going out, then that outlet is at the end of its particular circuit.

Some newer outlets or other fixtures may have push-in contacts rather than screws. The wire is pushed into a small hole far enough for a spring-loaded clamp to grip it. To release such a connection, insert the tip of a small screw-driver into the release hole and pull on the wire. These fixtures are clearly marked as to which side is the "white side."

Switches: Electrical switches are generally mounted in the same type of box used for outlets. If there are four wires in the box, two black and two white, the white wires will usually be connected to each other, and the two black wires will be connected to the switch. In another case, called the "switch leg," there are only two wires coming into the box. In this case, one wire is usually white and the other is black.

They are treated as if both were black, and the two are wired to the switch.

Most switches used in the home are toggle switches, and it is standard to mount them so that the electricity is on when the switch is in the up position. Silent mercury switches must be mounted in this position or they will not work. Mercury switches contain a small amount of mercury that flows to the lower end of the switch and completes the circuit when the switch is moved to the up position.

Wall and Ceiling Fixtures: Lights and other fixtures on the walls or ceilings of a home are also mounted on boxes. These boxes are larger than those used for outlets or switches, and are square in shape. Fixture boxes have the corners knocked off, so that they are actually eight-sided. Two opposing corners have screw holes. A metal bar or mounting plate is screwed into these holes, and runs diagonally across the box. The fixture is mounted to this bar.

Two wires, one white and one black, come into the fixture box. The fixture itself has two similar wires, and like colored wires are connected. Since the wires coming into the box are solid and the fixture wires are usually multi-strand, it can be difficult to make a strong splice. For a good connection, twist the two wires of the same color around one another and wrap the connection with electrician's tape, wrapping down over about an inch of insulation. A plastic wire nut may also be used, giving the connection both insulation and strength. Wire nuts are available at any hardware store. They simply twist on over a twisted pair of wires.

LAMPS

A lamp is a fairly simple piece of equipment. It has few parts that can break, and they are relatively easy to replace.

The first steps in dealing with a malfunctioning lamp are the obvious: make sure that the lamp is plugged in, that the bulb is not burned out, and that there is power to the outlet.

If the lamp still does not work, check the plug. Examine the plug for damage and the wires for fraying or looseness. If there appears to be damage here, replace the plug. There will be a screw on the bottom of the plug or a catch or release of some kind that will allow you to get at the wire connections on the inside of the plug. The wires are generally held in place by a pair of screws. Simply loosen the screws, pull the wires out, and connect them to the new plug.

The other thing that can be inspected quickly and easily is the contact at the bottom of the socket. With the lamp unplugged, remove the light bulb and examine the contact, a springy piece of metal mounted inside the socket. If the contact, a flexible strip of metal, is flat against the bottom, bend it up gently with a screwdriver. Replace the bulb and see if the lamp will work.

The next step is to disassemble the lamp. A lamp has a central support tube, threaded at each end, with the wire running through the tube. A retaining nut screws on to the bottom of the tube, and the lamp socket screws onto the top. At the bottom of the socket is a bracket that holds the harp, the curved wire support that holds the lamp shade. (Some small lamps have a shade that clamps directly on the bulb.) The cord, which runs through the support tube, is connected to the socket, which also contains the switch.

Since the switch is the only moving part of the lamp, it is the most likely thing to break. The switch is an integral part of the socket, and if the switch breaks, the entire socket must be replaced. Lamp sockets are standardized, but they do come in two sizes. The regular size takes standard light bulbs, and the larger size takes mogul-base bulbs, usually higher-powered three-way bulbs. These are usually used only in floor lamps.

To replace the socket, unplug the lamp and remove the bulb. On the side of the socket you will see the word *press*. Press hard on this point while pulling the round sleeve of the socket away from the cap, which is connected to the central tube of the lamp. If there is a paper insulating tube remaining on the cap, remove it. The interior workings of the socket are now exposed. Loosen the two connecting screws and disconnect the wires. Attach the new socket to the lamp by reversing the steps above.

If the new socket parts do not fit into the old cap, you will have to replace that too. Loosen the small setscrew that holds the cap on the central tube and unscrew the cap. Screw the new cap on and replace the rest of the socket parts. In attaching the wires to the new socket, twist the strands of the wire together in a clockwise direction and bend the wire in a U-shape. Hook the ''U'' over the screw and tighten.

CHAPTER
4

· · · · · · · · · · · · ·

Small Appliances

Household repairs on small household appliances are usually relatively quick and easy. Appliance malfunctions generally fall into one of three categories: minor (do-it-yourself), major (call the repairman), and disastrous (scrap it and get a new one). A little work with a broken appliance will usually let you know if you can fix it, and with practice you will soon be able to tell if it can be fixed, even by a professional.

If an appliance does not work at all, there are two very simple, but often overlooked, possible explanations that should be checked out first. First, make sure that the appliance is plugged in. Second, make sure that the outlet has power. Try another appliance in that outlet, or try the nonfunctioning appliance in an outlet that you know has power.

If you are going to be doing any repairs on electrical appliances, it is a good idea to put together a collection of the proper tools and supplies. Make sure that all the tools you use have insulated handles. In addition to normal screwdrivers and pliers, a multipurpose electrician's tool is very useful for stripping insulation from wires and for crimping electrical connectors. These tools are often sold in a kit with a collection of various connectors and fasteners. You should also have a roll of black electrical tape and, for more advanced repairs, solder and a soldering iron.

Two specialized instruments that come in handy in doing electrical repairs are a multitester and a continuity tester. A multitester is a metered device that indicates if a circuit is completed, as well as measuring the resistance of the circuit and the voltage. The continuity tester is a simpler, and less expensive device that indicates if a circuit is completed.

The simpler repairs for small appliances usually involve such things as broken plugs, frayed cords, or faulty switches. For anything more serious than this, particularly with inexpensive household appliances, it is often more economical to replace the unit rather than to try to fix it. Before attempting to fix any appliance, first check to see if it is still under warranty. Second, read the owner's manual and check for specific instructions on repair and disassembly. If a part is worn, bent, or otherwise damaged, it will generally have to be replaced. Always replace an appliance part with the same part from the manufacturer or from an authorized service center.

Disassembly of some small appliances is simple and obvious, while others are difficult, requiring some detective work to find screws or other fasteners. If the screws are not immediately apparent, run your fingers over any labels, particularly on the bottom, feeling for screwheads. Screws may be under rubber feet or pop-out plugs on the bottom, or they may be found by prying off a nameplate on the top.

If the appliance does no appear to have any screws or other fasteners, it may be held together by some kind of tabs or catches. If you have an appliance with no apparent screws, and the body is plastic and has a seam around it, try working a small screwdriver into the seam and prying it apart. Locate the tabs or catches and release them by pressing down on them with the blade of the screwdriver.

Replacing the Plug: A common problem with appliances, particularly small ones, is a defective plug. The plug casing may be cracked or broken, or the prongs of the plug may be bent or even broken off. Cracked or broken plugs should be replaced immediately.

Check the plug for a retaining screw of some kind. If there is one, loosen it and slip the body of the cap off the wire. If there is no retaining screw, look for a gap in the plug where the two parts of the plug can be pried apart. If there is no gap, it is a molded single-piece plug and it cannot be easily taken apart. In that case, simply cut the wire as close to the plug as possible.

After removing the old plug, either by loosening the screws on the inside of the plug casing or by snipping off the old plug, make sure that there is enough insulation stripped from the wires to fit the new plug, and that each wire is twisted to form a solid strand and bent to fit around the screws of the new plug. Insert the wires through the cap of the new plug, hook the wires around the screws, and tighten. Snap the new plug closed and you are all set.

Replacing the Cord: Any appliance cord that is frayed or cut, particularly if the wire is showing, should be replaced immediately. You may be able to find a replacement cord for the specific appliance. If not, look for a replacement cord designed for small appliances. This cord will already have a plug attached, so all you will have to do is remove the old cord and put on the new one.

Disassemble the appliance as much as necessary to expose the cord terminals. Disconnect the cord and remove it. The wires will usually be connected to their terminals with screw-on connectors. The cord may be held to the body of the appliance by a strain-relief grommet. If so, squeeze the grommet with a pair of needle-nose pliers and push it free.

Run the new power cord through the proper hole in the chassis. Replace the grommet if there is one, using a needle-nose pliers to push the grommet back into the hole in the body of the appliance. Connect the new cord to the terminals and reassemble the appliance.

TOASTERS

With proper care, there is little to go wrong with a toaster. Clean the toaster regularly, making sure that you unplug it first. Also, always unplug a toaster before attempting to free a stuck piece of bread or other food.

The carriage is the mechanism that holds the bread, lowering it into the toaster when you press down on the knob and popping it back up when the bread is toasted. If the carriage does not lower smoothly when you press down on the knob, or if it pops back up immediately, either the carriage mechanism or the latch is probably dirty and should be cleaned.

With the toaster cooled and unplugged, turn it upside down and open and remove the crumb tray on the bottom. Remove the knob by pulling it off or unscrewing it. The side of the toaster with the knob is called the latch panel. Remove this panel and you will have access to the latch assembly.

Use a sponge, a washcloth, or a paper towel over a screwdriver blade to remove crumbs and other deposits inside the toaster and sticking to the latch assembly. Hold the toaster over the sink and shake it to loosen debris stuck inside. Check the latch lever to see that it moves smoothly. If not, lubricate any moving parts, taking care not to get lubricant inside the toaster. Either slide a sheet of paper behind the latch assembly and spray the assembly with a spray lubricant, or spray the lubricant on a small cloth and wipe it on the moving parts. Let the lubricant set for a few minutes and wipe dry with a clean cloth, and recheck the mechanism.

If the latch doesn't catch, and the carriage won't stay down, the latch may be worn. Examine the latch hook and the latch release to see if the latch is slipping off rather than catching. If so, sharpen the worn parts of the latch so that it can hook on the release when it is pushed down.

If the toaster is popping up before the toast is done, even at the highest setting, or if the toast is overdone even at the lightest setting, the thermostat needs to be adjusted. Let the toaster cool and unplug it. Turn it upside down and remove the crumb tray. The thermostat bracket is mounted in a slot or rail in the bottom of the chassis, and slides in this slot. The ceramic thermostat tip itself is under or alongside the bracket. At one end of the slot is the solenoid switch, with wires leading to it from inside the chassis. As the thermostat tip moves closer to the solenoid switch, the toasting time gets shorter. Move the bracket away from the solenoid for a longer toasting cycle, and toward the solenoid for a shorter cycle. If the bracket does not slide relatively easily, it is held down by a screw or a rivet.

If there is a screw on the top of the bracket, loosen it, move the bracket in the desired direction, and tighten the screw. If the bracket is riveted, do not attempt to loosen or remove the rivet. The bracket can be moved with the rivet in place. Set the toaster on end, place the blade of a screwdriver against the bracket, and tap gently on the handle of the screwdriver with a hammer.

Close the tray and try the toaster. If the toast does not come out as desired, you will have to reset the thermostat again. Be careful not to move the thermostat tip closer than $3/16$ inch away from the outer contact of the solenoid switch.

If the toaster carriage does not stay down, or if it doesn't pop up when it should, the solenoid switch is probably faulty. If you have a multitester, you can test the switch to see if it is functioning properly. If it is faulty, if can be replaced. Remove the old solenoid by grinding off the rivet that holds it in place. Obtain a replacement from a dealer and mount it in the old rivet hole using a pop riveter. Reconnect the wires and reassemble the toaster.

STEAM IRONS

Modern steam irons are lighter than older models produced 15 to 20 years ago, and also usually have fewer replaceable parts. The electrical components of steam irons rarely malfunction. The most common problems are cut or frayed power cords and clogs in the water/steam system. Clogs are generally caused by inadequate cleaning. Most modern steam irons have a self-cleaning feature, usually activated by a button or lever on the side of the handle. Simply hold the hot iron over the sink and press the lever. Steam and water will spurt out of the bottom of the iron, as well as dirt and other deposits. The self-cleaning function should be used once a month.

If your steam iron does not have a self-cleaning function, it should be cleaned and flushed regularly. Start by heating the iron, and then unplugging it and letting it cool enough so that it can be handled. Use a small screwdriver or other small pointed instrument to scrap away any deposits around the steam ports, the holes in the soleplate or base of the iron. Many modern steam irons have soleplates coated with Teflon or other nonstick materials. Take particular care to avoid scratching the base of such an iron. If the soleplate is made of aluminum or stainless steel, remove residue or scratches by sanding the soleplate with a piece of very fine waterproof emery paper. Wrap the paper around a small block of wood, lightly dampen the soleplate, and sand the soleplate with smooth, even back-and-forth strokes. Wipe the soleplate with a clean damp cloth and polish it with 4/0 steel wool. Wipe off again with a damp cloth to remove any steel-wool particles.

Next, empty the water from the steam iron and refill it with a mixture of equal parts water and vinegar. Stand the steam iron in the sink and set the steam button to off. Plug in the iron, set it to its highest setting, and let it heat up for about 5 minutes. Unplug the iron, turn the steam button to on, and lay the iron flat in the sink. Leave the iron in the sink until all the water flows out. This may take as long as 10 minutes. Repeat this process two more times, using plain water.

Steam irons use a lot of power, up to 1000 watts for some models. Because of this, extra care should be taken with wiring. It is best not to use an extension cord with a steam iron. Under no circumstances use a household extension cord of the type commonly used for lamps or other small appliances. If it is absolutely necessary to use an extension cord, use a very heavy-duty model. An appliance with this kind of current consumption should be used with a 16-gauge extension cord at the very minimum, and the shorter the cord the better.

Replace steam-iron cords immediately if there is any sign of wear or damage to the outer insulation. The cord usually enters the iron through the top of the handle at the very back. The rear face of the handle assembly is called the back plate. It is usually held in place by a single screw. Unplug the steam iron and remove the back plate. Here you will see the power cord coming though the top of the handle, and the two wires connected to the main terminal posts of the iron. The wires may be connected with screws or twist-on connectors. Disconnect the wires and remove the old cord. Replace it with an equivalent cord, preferably a replacement part designated for that particular steam iron. Attach the wires to the main terminal posts and replace the back plate.

If the steam iron does not become hot enough, or if it becomes too hot or will not turn off, the thermostat is probably not set correctly. Correct calibration of the thermostat requires a multitester. Start with an unplugged steam iron at room temperature. Remove the back plate, and label and disconnect the wires from the main terminal posts. Connect a multitester probe to each main terminal post with the iron's control lever set to the off position. The multitester should indicate infinite resistance. If it doesn't, you will have to adjust the thermostat contacts.

On older-model steam irons, the thermostat contacts are under the saddle plate, which is the covering over the top of the main iron body. Pry the plate off gently with a small screwdriver, and the adjustment screw for the thermostat contacts will be underneath. On newer models, the thermostat contact adjustment screw is on top, near the temperature control lever. To reach it, turn the temperature control lever to the off position and push the temperature dial plate (the plate with the heat settings printed on it) back while slipping a screwdriver under the front edge. Pry up gently with the screwdriver to remove the plate. Under the plate are two screws. Remove the screws, turn the temperature control lever to the front, and pull up the handle plate. The thermostat contact adjustment screw will be under the handle plate, next to the temperature control lever.

Turn the adjustment screw clockwise, a quarter turn at a time, until the multitester indicates infinite resistance. Next, turn the temperature control lever to the lowest possible on position. The multitester should indicate about 12 ohms of resistance. If it does not, turn the adjustment screw a quarter turn counterclockwise, repeating until the multitester does indicate about 12 ohms. If the adjustment screw had to be turned more than a full turn for either adjustment, the iron should be serviced by a professional.

Many steam irons have a spray nozzle on the front, operated by a spray button on top of the handle. If there is little or no spray when the spray button is pumped, either the spray nozzle is clogged or the pump is clogged or leaking.

On older-model steam irons, the spray nozzle can be cleaned by removing the spray cap on the front of the iron. With the iron unplugged and cool, unscrew the spray cap, using a needle-nose pliers to loosen it if necessary. Beneath the cap is a small plug called the spreader, and a washer. Remove both and unscrew the nut that holds the front plate in place.

Using a fine needle, gently remove any deposits in or around the hole of the spray cap, being careful not to enlarge the hole. Replace the washer if it is dried out, and replace any other parts that are cracked or damaged. Reassemble the spray-nozzle assembly and clean the iron as described above.

On newer models, turn the temperature control lever to the off position and push the temperature dial plate (the plate with the heat settings printed on it) back while slipping a screwdriver under the front edge. Pry up gently with the screwdriver to remove the plate. Under the plate are two screws. Remove the screws, turn the temperature control lever to the front, and pull up the handle plate.

The spray button sits on the top of the actual pump. The pump is connected by a small hose to the spray nozzle, which rests in a hole in the front of the iron body. Pull the spray nozzle free of the hole and clean the nozzle of any deposits. Use a fine needle, taking care not to enlarge the nozzle opening. Next, pull out the temperature control lever, the spray button, and the steam button and its attached rod. A small screw holds the pump bracket in place. Remove the screw and hold the steam valve shaft steady while sliding the pump out from under its bracket.

Test the pump by placing it in a container of water and pressing down on the lever a few times. If the pump does not squirt water, clean it by soaking in vinegar for about 30 minutes. Test it again. If it still will not squirt water, or if the pump leaks, replace it with an exact replacement part. Reassemble the steam iron by reversing the steps.

HAIR DRYERS

A hair dryer is a relatively simple appliance, consisting of a fan, a heat element, and one or more switches to control the heat and fan speed. Most hair dryers have a built-in thermostat that shuts the hair dryer off if it overheats. If the hair dryer quits while in operation, or if you turn it off after long use and it won't turn back on right away, this is probably the cause. Let the hair dryer cool for a period and try it again. Overheating may be caused or worsened by dirt or hair inside the hair dryer.

Any kind of servicing of a hair dryer requires disassembly. The hair-dryer body usually consists of two mirror-image halves, held together by a few small screws or by internal clips or tabs. Some models require that the nozzle be slipped off before the body can be disassembled. The nozzle may also be held to the body by a screw or a clip. If there are no visible screws, and if you cannot slip a screwdriver blade into the seam between the body halves, the hair dryer is probably glued together. This usually means that the particular dryer is not serviceable.

Minor problems may be corrected with a simple cleaning. Remove the screws or pry the internal clips or tabs apart with a small screwdriver. Hold the hair dryer in one hand with the switch facing up, and remove the housing half that faces up. Clean the inside of the dryer, using an old toothbrush to remove hair, lint, and other debris. Lift off the fan housing and clean the fan. Check to see that the fan turns freely on its shaft. If it doesn't, check for hair or dirt tangled up around the fan shaft.

If the hair dryer works on only one heat setting or on only one fan-speed setting, it probably has a faulty switch. Testing and replacing switches usually requires a soldering iron and a continuity tester. Disassemble the hair dryer as discussed above. Test each switch by disconnecting one wire and attaching a continuity tester to the switch terminals. A wire may have to be desoldered to do this. The switch should show continuity in only one switch position. If the switch is faulty, replace it with the correct replacement part.

Any problems more complex than these usually require professional service, and it is generally less expensive to replace a hair dryer than to have it repaired.

FANS

Minor problems with household fans are easily fixed. If the motor goes bad, it is generally better to get a new fan. Many fans have a capacitor inside the motor housing. This is a batterylike device that stores power to allow the fan to operate smoothly. The capacitor can store dangerous voltage, and must be discharged before working on the internal parts of the fan. You can use a capacitor discharging tool, or you can make a simple device with a few basic parts. You will need two screwdrivers with insulated handles, two small jumper cables with alligator clips at each end, and a 20,000-ohm, two-watt resistor. These parts are commonly available at an electronics store. Clip a jumper cable to each screwdriver blade, and clip the other end of each jumper cable to a resistor lead.

Disassemble the fan to expose the capacitor, taking care not to touch it. Make sure that the fan has been unplugged for 5 to 10 minutes, and touch one of the screwdriver blades to each of the two capacitor terminals for a second or two. It is now safe to work on the internal parts of the fan.

If the fan is noisy or if it vibrates, start by checking to see that the fan is level and that it is on a padded surface. Check all clips and screws to see that they are properly tightened. Next, check to see if the fan blades are loose. With the fan unplugged, remove the blade guard. On an oscillating fan, pry the clips that hold the two halves of the blade guard together. On a box fan, remove the retaining screws that hold the front grille on the casing. Remove the spinner nut or setscrew that holds the blade assembly to the motor shaft. The spinner nut on a plastic blade assembly turns clockwise to loosen.

Slide the blade assembly off the motor shaft. Clean the blades with a damp cloth and inspect for cracks, warpage, or bends. Replace the blade assembly if necessary. Clean the motor shaft and reassemble the fan. If the fan blades turn sluggishly, follow the above disassembly and cleaning procedure. In addition, lubricate the fan bearings according to the directions in the owner's manual.

If an oscillating fan is jerky as it turns, you will need to check the gear assembly. Unplug the fan and remove the blade guard and the motor housing. Discharge the capacitor as discussed above, and remove it. The gearbox cover is behind the motor. Remove the screws and lift off the cover. Pull out the primary gear assembly, which is the main set of gears on top of the gearbox, and check for worn or broken gears. If the gears appear to be in bad shape, they should be replaced. If the secondary gears inside the gearbox are bad, you will have to take the fan in for professional service.

Clean all gears and remove any debris from inside the gearbox. Lubricate with a high-temperature grease, replace the primary gear assembly, and reassemble the fan.

MIXERS

The household mixer is a relatively simple device, consisting of a motor, gears, and a variable-speed switch. As with all electrical appliances, replace the cord if there is any damage to the outer insulation.

If the mixer vibrates badly and makes noise, first check the beaters to see if they are hitting one another or aren't turning properly. If so, examine the beaters to see if they are badly worn or if one or both are bent. If they are worn, or if they are bent and can't be straightened out, they will have to be replaced. If the beaters are okay, the trouble is probably in the gears.

Unplug the mixer and remove the beaters. Pull the switch knob off of its lever and turn the mixer over. Remove the screws from the bottom of the mixer body, called the motor housing. Hold the motor housing in one hand and the upper body housing in the other and work them apart.

Turn the motor housing upside down again and locate the small metal retaining rings and flat washers around the bottom of the gear spindles. Pry these off with a needle-nose pliers or a small screwdriver. Turn the motor housing right side up again and remove the switch assembly from the top front of the unit. You will now have access to the gears.

You will see a worm gear coming out from the motor, and a large pinion gear on either side of the worm gear. Pull up the pinion gears and remove them. Examine the pinion gears for cracks, wear, or other damage. If either gear is damaged in any way, replace both at the same time. Clean the inside of the gearbox with a clean dry cloth, and clean the worm gear with an old toothbrush.

Set the new gears in place and hold them there with your fingers while you tip the motor housing up and put the beaters in place. The beaters should intersect at a 45-degree angle, so that the blade of one is centered in the angle between two blades of the other. If the beaters are not properly aligned, remove one beater and lift out and rotate its gear. Put the beater back in to check the alignment. When the beaters are set at the proper angles, replace any clips or other fasteners that held down the gears. Lubricate the gears using a high-temperature grease, and reassemble the mixer.

BLENDERS

The typical household blender has two major components: the blender itself and a removable jar or pitcher to hold the food or liquid to be blended. The food container usually has a screw-on bottom unit, containing the blender blades, and a lid or cover, often with an opening through which further ingredients may be added. The blender base contains the motor and the controls, usually in the form of push buttons covering a range of speeds.

Inspect the food container regularly, particularly when cleaning it, looking for cracks in the jar or cover, bent blender blades, or a worn seal between the bottom of the jar and the blade assembly. Replace any damaged parts. Lubricate the blade assembly regularly with mineral oil. Do not use grease or machine oil on this or any other parts that come in contact with food.

If the blender overheats, or if the motor hums and the blades turn slowly or not at all, the blender is probably overloaded. Remove some of the food from the jar and try the blender again.

If the blender vibrates noisily, first check the blade assembly. If the blades are bent or damaged, replace the assembly. If the noise and vibration continues, check the drive stud. This is the shaft that sticks up from the base of the blender and transfers power to the blade assembly in the food jar. Inspect the drive stud for wear and for looseness.

If the drive stud is worn, it should be replaced. Turn the blender over and remove the screws that hold the bottom or base to the main housing. Find the motor shaft, which comes straight down from the motor. (You may have to remove the cooling fan blades to get access to the motor shaft.) Hold the motor shaft stationary with a wrench while turning the drive stud with another wrench. Remove the drive stud and the slinger, the large seal under the drive stud that prevents food from leaking into the base of the blender. Clean the slinger and the washer under it, replacing any worn parts. Reassemble the blender in reverse order.

If the blender doesn't run at some speeds, or even not at all, you should clean or replace the switch. Follow the instructions above to remove the base from the housing. On the front of the housing is a nameplate, which can be pried off with a small screwdriver or a knife. Remove the nameplate and loosen the screws found underneath it. Turn the housing over and pull out the switch assembly. Clean the switch thoroughly, using an old toothbrush and a damp cloth.

Each button on the switch is on the end of a shaft that slides up and down in an opening in the switch assembly. Spray electrical contact cleaner into each opening, at the same time pushing the button down several times. If any button sticks after cleaning, the switch will have to be replaced. Label and remove the wires, and replace the switch with a new one.

FOOD PROCESSORS

Food processors are more sophisticated and more complex versions of the blender. There are two basic designs: direct drive and belt drive. The belt-drive food processor is a larger, heavy-duty model, with a much larger capacity for processing food. Most food-processor problems are caused by improper use, and are usually solved by thorough cleaning. Proper care and cleaning of the unit will avoid most problems.

Older-model food processors may have a capacitor inside the motor housing. As with any appliance, unplug the unit before working on it. Disassemble the food processor carefully, checking for a capacitor. If there is a batterylike device mounted near the motor, do not touch it, either with your hand or with a tool. Read the instructions for dealing with capacitors in the section above that discusses fans.

If your food processor is noisy or vibrates excessively, first check the blade assembly to see if the blades are dirty, or if they are worn or bent. Clean the blades well, and replace them if they are damaged at all. If the noise or vibration continues, check the drive shaft that comes up from the base of the food processor and turns the blade assembly.

For a direct-drive food processor, remove the food bowl and examine the drive shaft. If it appears worn or if it spins freely by hand, it should be replaced. Pry the shaft up with a screwdriver. There will be a spring washer under the shaft that will also come up at this time. If the shaft appears to be in good shape, clean it thoroughly and put it back on the gear shaft.

On a belt-driven food processor, the shaft that turns the blade assembly is called the spindle shaft. To service this part, turn the unit on its side, remove the screws, and take off the lower housing. This will expose the drive belt and the drive assembly. The drive belt loops around the large drive wheel under the bowl and around the small motor pulley. On the outside of the belt is a bearing or wheel, mounted on an adjustable bracket, which pushes in on the belt to maintain tension. Loosen but do not remove the screw that holds this bearing bracket secure, and remove the belt. Inspect the belt, and replace it if shows any sign of wear or fraying.

There is a lock nut around the bottom of the spindle shaft, holding the shaft to the center of the large drive wheel. Pry this washer off with a screwdriver. Remove the drive wheel and the washer under it. Then pull the spindle shaft out from the top. Clean the spindle shaft thoroughly and inspect it for wear or damage. Replace it if there is any damage.

Reassemble the food processor, taking care to adjust the tension on the drive belt. Reinstall the belt and move it by hand. It should move smoothly. If it slips off the drive wheel or motor pulley, adjust the bearing bracket to increase the tension. If the belt is difficult to turn, decrease the tension.

If the blades of your belt-driven food processor change speed erratically, slowing down and speeding up, either the belt tension is not correctly set, or the belt is worn. Follow the instructions above for accessing the spindle shaft and check the belt. If adjusting the tension does not correct the problem, the belt should be replaced.

Overheating is usually caused by an overloaded bowl. Remove part of the contents of the bowl and allow the unit to cool. Continued overheating may be caused by a clogged air-intake screen. Thoroughly clean the screen in the lower housing, taking the unit apart if necessary. If the food processor still overheats, the motor is probably faulty.

VACUUM CLEANERS

There are two basic kinds of vacuum cleaners: canister and upright. Both use a motor-driven fan to create suction, pulling dirt into the machine and trapping it in a bag. The upright vacuum has a dirt fan that actually passes the dirt into the dirt bag. The canister model has the fan behind the dirt bag. The suction created by the fan draws air and dirt into the bag, where the dirt is trapped before it can reach the fan.

The first thing to check on a malfunctioning vacuum cleaner of either type is that the air passage is not clogged with dirt or other debris. With either type, make sure that the bag is not full. With a canister-type vacuum cleaner, also make sure that the hose or other attachments are clear of debris.

Many models of canister-type vacuum cleaners use disposable air filters in addition to bags. If the replacement bags for your particular model are packaged with small paper filter, find out how to install them, and use them. Other models have a permanent filter made of cloth or foam. These filters should be washed regularly.

If your vacuum cleaner shuts off after running for a time, the most likely problem is an overheated motor caused by a full bag or a dirty filter. Clean the vacuum cleaner thoroughly and allow it to cool before trying it again.

If your vacuum cleaner will not pick up dirt from any surface, check the bag, filter, and hoses as mentioned above. If the problem seems to center around cleaning carpets, there may be something wrong with the beater bar.

The beater bar is a rotating drum with attached brushes at

the front of the vacuum cleaner. The drum turns and vibrates at high speed to get the dirt from deep in a carpet. The beater-bar brushes may be clogged with hair or other debris, so that the brushes are no longer properly bringing the dirt up from the pile of the carpet. Check the brushes on the beater bar, and remove all hair, dirt, and other debris. You may have to use a screwdriver or other pointed tool to work some of this debris out of the brush bristles.

For heavy-duty cleaning of the beater bar, remove the bottom plate of the upright vacuum cleaner or of the power head of the canister-type cleaner. Disengage the drive belt and pull out the beater bar. Clean the beater bar thoroughly and lubricate the bearings. If the brushes on the beater bar are worn, they should be replaced. Twist off the end plate of the beater bar and pry off the inner metal flange with a screwdriver. Hold the end of the brush with your hand or with a pair of pliers, and pull it out of the slot in the beater bar. Slide new brushes into the slot and reassemble the parts in reverse order.

The beater-bar drive belt often slips off or breaks, particularly if something gets clogged in the beater bar. Make sure that the replacement part is the correct one. To replace the belt on an upright vacuum cleaner, slide the belt into the groove in the beater bar, snap the bar into place, and loop the belt around the motor pulley. On a canister-type vacuum cleaner, first loop the belt around the drive shaft of the power nozzle and then around the groove in the beater bar, which is still out of its mounting slots. Finally, push the beater bar back into the mounting slots. This may require a lot of force.

Failure to clean carpets properly may also be caused by a beater bar that is set too high or too low on an upright model. The beater-bar height is set by adjustments to the wheels of the upright vacuum cleaner. Check your owner's manual for instructions on setting the correct height.

Excessive noise or vibrations can be caused by a number

of things. One possible cause is a loose or broken drive belt. Follow the procedures above for cleaning the beater bar to check out the drive belt. At the same time, check to see if the beater bar is loose. The clips that hold the beater bar in place may be loose or worn. If necessary, replace these clips. If all of the above fail, the motor-shaft bearing is probably worn. This generally requires professional service.

ELECTRIC SHAVERS

Electric shavers fall into two general categories: foil head and rotary head. The major maintenance jobs for electric shavers are cleaning and replacing the cutter assemblies. Most electric shavers also have trimmers, which can become dull or need service. Since many modern electric shavers are rechargeable, the battery-recharger system is another potential source of malfunction.

If the shaver does not run at all, the first things to check are that the shaver is plugged in, that the outlet has power, and that any batteries are charged. If a rechargeable shaver needs frequent recharging, or if it runs out of power before you can even complete a shave, either the rechargeable batteries or the battery charger are faulty. Have these tested by a professional, and replace them if necessary.

Foil-Head Shavers: A foil-head shaver is shaped like a small oblong box, with a head assembly that holds the screen and the trimmer. The cutter assembly is under the screen. This consists of a number of small blades that vibrate against the screen to cut the hair. If the shaver grabs or pinches, examine the screen for any corrosion or damage. Replace the screen if necessary, by removing the head assembly and prying the screen out of the assembly with a small screwdriver.

If the shaver gives a rough or uneven shave, the cutter

blades may be dull, or the head assembly may be damaged. Either should be replaced if needed. The head assembly either pulls right off or is released via a small button on the side of the shaver. The main cutter assembly is removed by giving it a partial turn to one side or the other and pulling it off of the cutter arm. On the underside of the cutter is the carrier. Pry this off with a small screwdriver. Snap the new cutter onto the carrier, and then slide the carrier back onto the cutter arm.

The trimmer blade is generally built into the head assembly, and this assembly should also be replaced if the trimmer grabs or cuts unevenly. If the trimmer is noisy, the trimmer blades should be lubricated.

If the motor seems to run okay but the shaver doesn't work, or if it is excessively noisy, most likely the oscillators are worn and need to be replaced. There are two oscillators, one for the cutting blades and one for the trimmer. These parts transmit motion from the motor to the blades, causing them to oscillate and to cut hair. To gain access to the oscillators, first remove the head assembly and the cutter as discussed above. Then loosen any screws securing the back of the shaver to the housing and remove the back. There may be one or more screws under small plastic plugs that need to be pried out with a very small screwdriver.

Under the back cover is the motor and circuit-board assembly. This assembly has a motor shaft that goes up through a hole in the bottom of the oscillators. Lift the motor and circuit-board assembly and twist it sideways to free the motor shaft.

There is a rubber hair stopper over the oscillators that should be removed. The cutter oscillator sits on top of the trimmer oscillator. Slide the cutter oscillator out of its slots in the top of the housing, followed by the trimmer oscillator. If either is worn, replace it with a duplicate part.

Rotary-Head Shavers: A rotary-head shaver has one or

more combs or circular screens, each with a rotating cutter underneath. Each cutter has a number of small blades that cut hair as the cutter rotates under the comb. The cutters and combs are held in their proper position by the bracket, which in turn is attached to the shaver head. The shaver head then snaps onto the shaver.

If the shaver shaves unevenly or if the heads slow down while you shave, the first step is to lubricate the combs and cutters by spraying on a factory-recommended lubricant while the shaver is running. If that does not take care of the problem, replace the combs and cutters. To replace the combs and cutters, simply pull the shaver head off the shaver, and then follow the instructions provided with the replacement set.

Most rotary-head shavers have a pop-up trimmer. If the trimmer grabs or cuts unevenly, the trimmer blade should be replaced. To access the trimmer, unscrew and remove the back cover. Pop the trimmer into cutting position and inspect it for damage or dullness. If it is necessary to replace the trimmer, pry one corner of the trimmer assembly out of the cover with a small screwdriver. Snap the replacement part into place.

If the shaver is excessively noisy or vibrates badly, the gears need lubrication or are worn. Remove the shaver head, and then unscrew and remove the back cover. The gear cover, located under the shaver head, is held in place by three plastic retaining tabs. Two of these tabs can be released from the rear with a small screwdriver. The third tab is then released by pulling up on the front of the gear cover.

Clean the gears thoroughly, removing the larger gears by pulling them straight up. There is one large gear for each cutter and a central pinion gear that turns the others. Check the pinion gear to see that it is not worn or damaged. If it is, pry it up with a very small screwdriver and replace it. If the large gears are worn or damaged, replace them. Put a drop of light oil on each gear pin and replace the gears. Snap on the gear cover and reassemble the shaver.

CAN OPENERS

Many can openers also have the ability to sharpen knives and scissors. Problems with can openers usually involve either the cutter mechanism that actually opens the can or the sharpening mechanism. Regular cleaning, particularly of the cutter mechanism, will avoid a lot of problems. Always unplug the can opener before cleaning it or working on it. Never immerse the can opener in water, although the lever arm can be removed and washed in soap and water.

A thorough cleaning of the cutter assembly usually requires removal of the lever arm. This is the operating arm that activates the can opener. Examine the lever arm to determine if it is held in place by one or more screws. If so, loosen the screws and remove the arm. If there are no screws apparent, lift the arm all the way up and slide it to one side to slip it out of the key-shaped hole it is mounted in, and pull the arm forward.

Clean the cutter mechanism thoroughly, including any gears or other accessible parts that have food or dirt built up. If the cutter appears worn or damaged, or if the can opener still does not work well after cleaning, the cutter should be replaced. The cutter is attached to the lever arm, and can be easily removed while the lever arm is off the can opener.

Under the lever arm, and easily accessible while the arm is off, is the feed gear. This is a wheel with gear teeth that grip the rim of the can and feed the can through the cutter mechanism. Keep the feed gear clean, and replace it if it is worn or damaged. If the can opener will not hold a can tightly, the feed gear may be worn or out of alignment. The space between the cutter and the feed gear should be no wider than the thickness of a piece of paper. If the gap is larger than this, the feed gear needs to be shimmed with an appropriate-size washer.

For access to the feed gear, loosen the screws that hold on the back cover of the can opener and remove the back. Inside the front housing is a large gear, called the spur gear, that is on the same shaft as the feed gear. Hold the spur gear steady, either by grasping it with a cloth or by holding it in place with a screwdriver if it has a hole or a slot in it. While holding the spur gear steady, put a small piece of cloth over the feed gear to prevent damage and unscrew it with a pair of pliers or channel locks. Replace the feed gear or shim it with a washer and reassemble the can opener.

If the can does not turn when the lever arm is pushed down, but the feed gear does turn, then the feed gear needs to be cleaned or replaced. If the can does not turn and the feed gear does not turn either, then the idler gear probably needs replacement. Unscrew and remove the back of the unit. The idler gear is usually located between the motor and the spur gear. The spur gear is on the inside of the unit, on the same shaft as the feed gear.

Move the motor aside carefully and pull the idler gear off of its shaft. On some models the spur gear is on top of the idler gear. In that case, remove the feed gear as discussed above, and then remove the spur gear and the idler gear. Inspect the idler gear for wear or damage and replace it if necessary. Clean out the inside of the can opener, apply grease to the gear shaft, and reassemble the unit.

HUMIDIFIERS

The two basic types of humidifiers are the ultrasonic and the evaporative styles. Evaporative humidifiers are either of the drum type or the rotating-pad type. In either of the evaporative humidifiers, a moving filter picks up water, passing in front of an electric fan that blows dry air through it and out into the room. The ultrasonic humidifier works electronically by breaking up molecules of water and turning them into mist, which is released into the room.

Evaporative Humidifiers: Evaporative humidifiers have filters and reservoirs that should be cleaned regularly. The rotating-pad humidifier has a filter pad in the shape of a wide endless belt. The pad is mounted on two rollers that rotate the pad in front of the fan. The pad and roller assembly is mounted in a frame that slides into channels in the sides of the reservoir.

To remove the pad, take the top off the humidifier, remove any screws holding the frame to the reservoir, and pull the frame up and out. Lay the frame on newspaper or a tarp spread on the floor. Release the bottom roller by pulling the frame sides apart and slipping the roller out. The top roller is held in place by a bearing with a thumbscrew-type handle. Turn the bearing clockwise until it is vertical and pull it out. This will free the top roller.

Slide the pad off the rollers, and inspect the rollers for wear or damage. Replace the rollers if necessary. Soak the pad in a mixture of equal parts water and vinegar. Rinse it thoroughly under running water. If the pad is badly stained or contains mineral deposits that cannot be cleaned, replace the pad. Fill the reservoir with the same solution of water and vinegar, allowing it to stand for an hour or two. Scrub the reservoir with a stiff brush and rinse well. Put the pad back on the rollers and reassemble the humidifier.

To clean a drum-type humidifier, open the lid and lift the drum, pulling it forward at the same time that you lift. Lay the drum on newspapers or a tarp spread out on the floor. If the filter belt is a single piece, slide it off the drum. If there is a plastic belt retainer between the ribs of the drum, pry out the retainer and release the ends of the filter belt. Soak the filter belt in a mixture of equal parts water and vinegar, and rinse well under running water. Replace the filter belt on the drum while it is still wet.

While the filter belt is soaking, remove any screws and lift the power pack, the motor and fan assembly, out of the body of the humidifier. Next lift out the reservoir, which may still contain water. Fill the reservoir with a mixture of equal parts water and vinegar and let stand for an hour or two. Rinse out the reservoir and reassemble the humidifier.

Evaporative humidifiers have a float mechanism that turns the machine off if there is no water in the reservoir. If the humidifier does not work and it does have power, the next step is to see that there is water in the reservoir. If there is water, check to make sure that the float mechanism is indeed floating on the water. If the float is in water but is underwater, replace the float. If the humidifier still does not work, the switches or even the motor may be faulty.

If the motor and the fan both run but the filter does not turn, check the belt drive to see if it is loose or broken. Unplug the humidifier and open the lid. Belt-drive access varies from model to model. On rotating-pad types, you will have to remove the pad frame, and then you may have to disengage the transmission shaft and lift out the drive box. On drum-type humidifiers, remove the drum and the power pack for access to the drive belt. Examine the belt for wear, damage, or signs of slipping. If necessary, slip the drive belt off of its pulleys and replace it with a new one.

Ultrasonic Humidifiers: An ultrasonic humidifier vibrates water at an ultrasonic frequency. An oscillating disk, called the transducer, breaks up the water molecules into a water vapor, which is mixed with air, and the resulting fine mist is released into the room. Minerals in hard water may appear as a fine white dust in the room where the ultrasonic humidifier is used, and these minerals may also appear as mineral deposits in the humidifier itself. Clean the unit according to the owner's manual to minimize this problem. If the problem is too bad, use distilled water in the humidifier.

With proper care, there are few things to go wrong with an ultrasonic humidifier. If the humidifier is emitting air from the nozzle but no water mist, check to see that the controls are set properly and that there is water in the tank. If there is still no water mist, the problem is probably with the transducer.

The upper part of the humidifier consists of the water tank and the mist chamber. Remove the water tank and the mist chamber, and fill the reservoir under the mist chamber with water. Turn the humidifier on to the highest setting and check to see if the water in the reservoir agitates. If the water does not agitate, there is a problem with an electronic component and the humidifier should be taken in for service. If the water agitates but no mist is produced, the problem is with the transducer.

Unplug the humidifier and empty the reservoir. Turn the humidifier over, loosen the screws on the bottom, and remove the base plate. The transducer is a relatively flat, oblong device, wired to the circuit board and mounted so as to protrude through the housing into the reservoir. Disconnect the two wires from the transducer, remove the mounting screws, and pull out the transducer. Buy an exact replacement part from a dealer.

Apply a bead of silicon adhesive around the hole in the mounting plate and press the transducer down into the hole. Reassemble the unit, reversing the step above. Wait for about 24 hours, allowing the adhesive to dry, before using the unit.

CHAPTER
5
. . . .
Major Appliances

Major appliances include such household fixtures as refrigerators and stoves. Most are relatively simple devices, with few working parts that can break. The thing to keep foremost in mind at all times in working with these appliances is the potential danger from unsafe practices around gas and electricity. Before working on major gas appliances, make sure that the gas is turned off. Before working on any electrical appliance, make sure that either the electricity is turned off at the circuit panel or that the appliance is unplugged.

It is a very good idea to know ahead of time how to turn off the gas to your range or water heater, and where the circuit-breaker panel is and which breakers control which appliances. In the event of emergency, you will then be able to turn off the gas or electricity without wasting time locating the shutoff controls. It is also a good idea to know where the individual and main water valves are so that you can turn off the water if there is a plumbing problem with a washer or a water heater. If you ever do have a broken water pipe, and if an electrical appliance is standing in water, do not enter the room until you have turned off the electrical power to that appliance, or to the whole house if you are not sure which circuit supplies power to that particular appliance.

REFRIGERATORS

A refrigerator is a fairly simple machine. It consists of an insulated box with a refrigerant gas in a network of coils and a compressor. The compressor forces the refrigerant gas into condenser coils, increasing the pressure and causing the gas to give off heat. The gas then passes into the evaporator coils, which, being larger, reduce the pressure on the gas. As the gas loses pressure, it absorbs heat, cooling the area around the coils. The gas then returns to the compressor to start the cycle over again.

As far as the actual cooling process is concerned, as long as the compressor motor works and the refrigerant gas does not leak out, the refrigerator will work. Most of the problems with refrigerators are problems with gaskets, switches, or other peripheral devices.

Defrosting: Most modern refrigerators have some kind of device to prevent frost buildup. Frost buildup is inevitable, and is caused by moist air that enters the refrigerator when the door is open, condenses on the inside of the refrigerator, and turns to ice. The old-fashioned way to deal with frost buildup was to turn off the refrigerator and let the ice thaw enough so that it could be removed. Modern refrigerators solve the problem with some kind of defrosting heater that periodically warms the evaporator coils enough to melt the ice and let the water flow into an evaporating pan in the bottom of the refrigerator.

Frost-free refrigerators have defrosting heaters that remove the ice in both the freezer compartment and in the main refrigerator compartment. Semiautomatic refrigerators automatically defrost only the main refrigerator compartment. The freezer compartment must still be periodically defrosted manually. A manual refrigerator must be defrosted manually. Regular cleaning and defrosting prolongs the life of the refrigerator and lowers the energy bill.

To defrost a refrigerator or freezer manually, turn the thermostat to off or unplug it. Use a hair dryer or pans of hot water to thaw the built-up ice enough to pull it off the interior walls. Never attempt to chip the ice away with a sharp instrument. You will scratch the inside walls of the refrigerator, and you could puncture the evaporator coils. Thoroughly clean the refrigerator inside and out during the defrosting process. It is especially important to clean the coils that are located on the back or under the refrigerator. Clean coils cool more efficiently, lowering both the strain on the machine and the electricity bill. Vacuum the coils or clean them with a brush. If they are particularly dirty or greasy, wash them with hot soapy water. Make sure that the drains, drain tubes, and drain pans are cleaned regularly, or they could start to smell. Flush out the drain system with hot water and baking soda. Wash out the trays, shelves, and interior compartments every six months with hot water and baking soda.

Condenser coils: A number of refrigerator problems are caused by dirty condenser coils. Dirty coils can cause the compressor to overheat, shutting the refrigerator down. Dirty coils can also cause the refrigerator to start and stop rapidly or to run constantly. Check the coils first to see that they are clean if you are having any problems with your refrigerator.

If the coils are mounted on the back of the refrigerator, they should be cleaned at least once a year. Pull the refrigerator away from the wall and clean the coils with a brush or with a vacuum cleaner with a brush attachment. If the coils are under the refrigerator, pull off the grille at the bottom of the unit and use a vacuum cleaner with a long thin nozzle attachment to clean underneath.

Interior Light: The light on the inside of the refrigerator can be your first indication of potential problems. If the refrigerator does not run and the light does not come on (assuming that the bulb is not burned out), then there is no power to the refrigerator. Make sure that the refrigerator is plugged in and that the circuit breaker had not been tripped or the fuse been blown. Next, check to see if the power cord is loose or faulty.

Inoperative Refrigerator: If the light works but the refrigerator does not run, there are many things that could be wrong. First, check to see that the temperature control on the inside of the refrigerator is turned on. The next step is to test the temperature control. This requires a continuity tester. Temperature controls are either a simple dial type, with a single control, or the console type, with separate refrigerator and freezer controls.

For a dial-type temperature control, unplug the refrigerator, remove a screw in the center of the dial if there is one, set the dial to the coldest setting, and pull it straight off. Removing the dial exposes the temperature control itself. Remove the two screws holding the control to the inside wall of the refrigerator and pull the control out enough to expose a few inches of wiring. There will be a metal capillary line attached to the control. Take care not to bend this line.

Pull the wire connectors off the temperature control and attach a continuity-tester probe to each terminal of the temperature control. With the temperature control set at its coldest setting, the continuity tester should light. Next, twist the control shaft all the way in the other direction to the off position. The continuity-tester light should now be off. If the temperature control is faulty, replace it with a duplicate new part.

For a console-type temperature control, first remove the

console by unscrewing it or lifting it off of its catches. The temperature control will be mounted on the console while the freezer-vent control will remain mounted on the refrigerator wall. Unscrew and remove the freezer-vent control. Thaw and remove any ice, clean the freezer-vent control unit, and clean out the freezer channel in the refrigerator wall where the freezer-vent control was mounted. Remount the freezer-vent control.

The console will contain the temperature control, and if the refrigerator has one, an energy-saver switch. Remove the connectors from the energy-saver switch and check the switch for continuity. If the switch is faulty (if the continuity tester does not light when connected to the terminals) replace it with a duplicate part. The energy-saver switch should easily snap in and out of the console, and the wires should attach with push-on connectors.

Next, remove the push-on wire connectors from the temperature control and touch a continuity probe to each terminal. The continuity tester should light when the temperature control is set to its coldest setting, and it should not light when the control is set to the off position. If the temperature control is faulty, replace it with a duplicate part. Before removing the old temperature control, take note of the position of the capillary line in the console. This line is a part of the temperature control and will be removed with it. When installing the new control, make sure that the capillary line of the replacement part is installed in the same position.

Constant Running: If the refrigerator runs constantly, there are several things that could be wrong. First, check to see if there is excessive frost buildup. If so, defrost the refrigerator. If there is frost buildup in a frost-free refrigerator, particularly if there is a lot of ice in the bottom of the freezer, you may have a blocked drain or drain tube. Turn the refrigerator off and defrost it. Once you have removed the ice, rinse out the drain at the bottom of the freezer compartment and make sure that there are no obstructions or kinks in the drain tube.

Constant running may also be caused by the door failing to seal properly or by a faulty door gasket. Examine the door gasket for tears, cracks, or brittleness. If there is any damage, replace the gasket. Purchase a new door gasket from an appliance dealer and soak the new gasket in warm water while you remove the old one. Pull back the door gasket to expose the retaining strip. Loosen the screws and pull on the gasket. On newer models, the gasket will come right out. On older models, the screws pass through the gasket and will have to be removed.

Remove the gasket from the top half of the door only and begin to install the new gasket. Insert the back flange of the new gasket behind the retaining strip and partially tighten the screws. Then remove the rest of the old gasket and install the remainder of the new one. When the gasket is completely in place, tighten all the screws.

If the gasket did not need replacement, check the door on all sides for obvious gaps. Take a dollar bill and close the door on it. When pulling the bill out, you should feel some resistance. Repeat this test at various places around the door. If the door does not seal tightly, adjust the front feet or front rollers of the refrigerator to raise the front slightly. If the door still does not seal tightly, check the door for sagging or warping.

If the door appears to be sagging, with the hinge side of the door higher than the other side, adjust the door hinges. Loosen the hinges with a wrench and lift the edge of the door until it is square with the main body of the refrigerator. Hold the door in place and retighten the hinge bolts.

If the door is slightly warped, straightening the door with

the hinge bolts as discussed above may correct the problem. If the warpage is more severe, the door will have to be realigned. Open the door and pull back the door gasket to expose the retaining strip. Loosen but do not remove the screws in the strip. Hold the outer door panel at the top and at the side and apply pressure in the opposite direction of the warp. Hold the door in this position while a helper tightens the screws in the retaining strip.

Inadequate Cooling: If the refrigerator is not cold enough, there are several things to check. First, make sure that the temperature control is not set too high. Again, check to see that the condenser coils are not dirty, that there is no damage to the door gaskets, and that the door seals properly. Improper cooling can also be caused by ice buildup. Defrost the refrigerator if necessary. Next, if you have the proper equipment, check the temperature control as discussed above. If none of these actions solve the problem, you will have to call for professional help.

Excessive Noise: A noisy refrigerator also has several potential causes. The first thing to do is make sure that the refrigerator is level. Adjust the feet or rollers so that the refrigerator is high enough in the front that the door swings smoothly closed from a half-open position. Next, check the drain pan under the refrigerator to see that it is not rattling. If it is, simply move it slightly until it stops rattling while the refrigerator is running.

Noise can be caused by loose or damaged compressor mountings. Unplug the refrigerator and pull it away from the wall. If there is an access panel at the bottom of the refrigerator in the back, remove it. Check the nuts holding down the compressor mountings to see that they are tight. Also examine the shock-absorbing mounting under each foot of the compressor. If these mountings have hardened, they should be replaced. Remove the nut holding one foot of the compressor and lift the compressor up with a pry bar. Pull out the mounting and replace it. Replace and tighten the nut, and repeat the process for the other mountings, one at a time.

Noise can also be caused by damaged condenser or evaporator fans. Inspect these fans, and replace them if they are damaged.

ICE MAKERS

If the ice maker is not making ice, and if the refrigerator appears to be running properly and the freezer is cold enough, first check to see that the water supply to the ice maker is turned on. The water for the ice maker generally flows through a thin copper tube connected to the water pipes under the kitchen sink. Check the shutoff valve on this tube to make sure that it is not turned off.

If the valve is turned on and the ice maker is not getting water, the water-inlet valve may be faulty. Checking the water-inlet valve requires a multitester. Unplug the refrigerator and turn off the water supply to the ice maker. Pull the refrigerator away from the wall and locate the water-inlet valve on the back of the refrigerator where the copper water-supply tube terminates. Remove any screws holding the valve to the refrigerator and disconnect the tube sleeves from the valve ports. The tube sleeves are screw-on connectors, one from the copper water-supply tube and one to the refrigerator. These connections resemble small garden-hose connections.

Put a pan under the valve before disconnecting it, in order to catch any water in the tubes or the valve. Disconnect the wires attached to the water-inlet valve and pry out the filter in the inlet port and clean it. Set your multitester at RX10 and touch a probe to each terminal on the valve. If the tester does not show 200 to 500 ohms of resistance, replace the valve and reassemble the unit. If you have installed a new water-inlet valve, discard the first few batches of ice until the new valve is cleaned out.

If the ice maker will not stop making ice, check to see that the shutoff arm is properly adjusted. The shutoff arm is a long metal rod that is raised by the ice filling the ice bucket. When the arm gets high enough, it turns off the ice maker. If propping up the shutoff arm stops the ice maker, but it will not shut off otherwise, then the shutoff arm is not working properly.

Unplug the refrigerator and remove the ice maker. The ice maker is held in place with several screws and possibly some clips. Remove the screws and unplug the ice maker from the refrigerator wall. Pry the cover off the front of the ice-maker unit with a small screwdriver.

Check to see that the spring is engaged on the shutoff arm, and that the arm fits into the slot on the shutoff lever in the front housing of the ice maker. If the arm or spring were not properly engaged, install them properly, reassemble the ice maker, and see if it operates correctly.

To remove the shutoff arm, disengage the arm from the shutoff lever and push it forward, working it out of its mounting hole in the ice-maker housing. Slide a replacement arm through the hole in the front of the housing and reinstall the ice maker.

If the ice maker is not refilling when empty, first check to see that the water is turned on at the valve, which is usually located behind the refrigerator or under the kitchen sink. Next, check the water inlet valve to see if the filter is clogged. Turn off the water supply to the ice maker and pull the refrigerator away from the wall. The inlet valve is mounted on the back of the refrigerator, and is the terminating point for the small copper water-supply pipe. Unscrew the bracket that holds the valve to the refrigerator.

Place a small pan under the valve and remove the tube sleeves that connect the valve to the water supply and to the refrigerator. Disconnect the wires from the valve, pry the filter out of the valve with a small screwdriver, and rinse the filter in cold water. Test the valve solenoid with a multitester. Set the multitester at RX10 and touch the probes to the terminals of the solenoid. If the multitester does not indicate 200 to 500 ohms of resistance, the water-inlet valve is defective and should be replaced.

FREEZERS

Home freezers differ little from refrigerators in operation, and usually have fewer options or devices to go wrong. If your freezer is not an automatic-defrost model, you will have to defrost it when frost builds up, usually once or twice a year. Remove the food and allow the ice to thaw to the point where it can be removed without chipping. Speed up the process with a hair dryer or pans of hot water. Wash out the freezer with warm water and baking soda.

For maximum energy efficiency, allow hot foods to cool to room temperature before storing them in the freezer. Also, avoid locating the freezer near any major heat source, such as a clothes dryer, a furnace, or a water heater.

Freezers generally have a power indicator light mounted on the front of the cabinet. If the light is out and the freezer is not running, there is no power to the freezer. Check to see that the freezer is plugged in and that the circuit breaker is not tripped. If the light still does not come on, unplug the freezer and check the power cord to see if it is loose or defective. If so, tighten it or replace it.

If the power indicator light is not on but the freezer is running, either the light or the motor relay is faulty. To check the light, unplug the freezer and pry the light unit out of the front of the freezer cabinet with a small screwdriver. Disconnect the wires from the light, labeling them and taping them to the front of the cabinet so that they do not slip back inside. Check the light with a continuity tester. If the tester does not indicate continuity, install a new power indicator light.

To test the motor relay, first unplug the freezer. Some freezers are accessible directly from the back, while others have an access panel on the side which must be removed. The relay is under the terminal cover, a small boxlike appendage to the compressor. Use a screwdriver to pry the retaining clip off the terminal cover and remove the cover. The motor relay is plugged directly into pins on the compressor. Pull it straight off, label the wires, and disconnect them.

Some motor relays have a copper coil while others do not. If there is a copper coil, hold the relay with the word *top* facing up. Use a multitester set at RX1, attaching a probe to terminal "L" on the side of the relay and the other probe to terminal "M" on the top. The tester should indicate continuity.

Remove the probe from the "M" terminal and insert it into the "S" terminal. The tester should indicate resistance. With the probes in place, turn the motor relay upside down. You should hear a slight click, and the tester should change to indicating continuity. Next, move the probe from the "L" terminal to the "M" terminal. Again, the tester should indicate continuity. If the relay fails any of these tests, replace it with a new one.

If the motor relay does not have a copper coil, simply insert the probes of the multitester into the two terminals of the relay. The multitester should indicate 5 to 10 ohms of resistance. If it does not, replace the motor relay.

Excessive Noise: An excessively noisy freezer usually

indicates that the freezer is not level or that the compressor mountings are loose or have hardened. Level the freezer by adjusting the leveling feet. If the freezer does not have any, or if the feet do not adjust sufficiently to level the freezer, use wooden shims under the freezer to level it. If the freezer is still noisy, see how to tighten or replace compressor mountings in the section above dealing with refrigerators.

Constant Running: If the freezer runs constantly, either it needs to be defrosted or the door is not sealing properly. The door is sealed by the gasket on the door contacting with the breaker strips on the cabinet. To replace the breaker strips, unplug the freezer and open the door. Keep the contents of the freezer cold by covering with blankets, newspapers, or other insulating material. At each corner of the freezer chest is a corner bracket that holds in the breaker strips. You should be able to snap the brackets out with your hand. If you can't, warm them slightly with a hair dryer.

Snap out the breaker strips along the top of the cabinet with your hands. If the strips do not come out easily, pry them with a putty knife, covering the blade with a rag or tape to avoid damage. If the insulation under the breaker strips is dry, snap in new breaker strips. If the insulation is wet, it is best to store the frozen food and leave the insulation uncovered to dry.

To replace the door gasket, unplug the freezer and cover the contents with blankets or other insulation. Remove the freezer door and turn it upside down on the freezer. Soak a new gasket in warm water to loosen it. The gasket is held on with plastic studs or with screws. Remove the fasteners three or four at a time, pull out the old gasket, and put the new gasket in its place. Continue this way, working around the door until the new gasket is in place. If the gasket is held in place with screws, replace the screws loosely as you go, tightening them after the new gasket is installed.

ELECTRIC RANGES

The basic functions of an electric range are performed by a few simple components. There are usually four surface heating elements, each controlled by a switch, and an oven containing a baking element and a broiling element. These later elements are controlled by an oven selector switch and a temperature control switch. The typical modern range also has a clock, a timer for automatic baking, and an oven light. Many modern electric ranges are self-cleaning, with separate timers and a door-locking mechanism. Self-cleaning ovens clean by burning soil off at very high temperatures, and the door-locking mechanism is a safety precaution against opening the oven door when the oven is very hot during or immediately after the self-cleaning cycle.

It is important to use the range properly to avoid problems and malfunctions. Always use drip pans under the surface heating elements, and never line those drip pans with foil. Never line the bottom or the shelves of an oven with foil. And never clean the door gasket of a self-cleaning oven.

Inoperative Range: If nothing on the range works, the range is not getting power. This may be caused by a circuit breaker, by the range not being plugged in, by a faulty power cord, or by a faulty terminal block. If the circuit breaker is set and the range is plugged in, unplug the power cord and check to see if it is loose or damaged. If so, tighten or replace the power cord.

Next, check the terminal block. This is a small plug inside the appliance that connects the power cord to the internal wiring of the electric range. Pull the two parts of the plug apart and inspect the parts for signs of burning, cracking, or corrosion. Replace any damaged parts.

If all of the elements, either surface or oven, do not heat, or heat only partially, check the same items discussed above. This problem may be caused by a tripped circuit breaker (a major appliance such as an electric stove may be on more than one circuit breaker), by a faulty power cord, or by a faulty terminal block.

Inoperative Burner: If a surface element or burner does not heat, check to see that the element is properly seated in its receptacle. Modern burners are plug-in elements with terminals that slide into an electrical receptacle in the side of the burner opening on the top of the range. Turn the switch off, pull the element up and out of its receptacle, and then put the element back into its proper position.

If the burner still does not work, unplug the range, remove the element and drip pan, and unscrew the receptacle and pull it out, taking care not to strain the wiring. Some ranges require lifting the top to remove the receptacles. Examine the receptacle for signs of damage, including cracks and burning. Replace the receptacle if it appears damaged in any way.

An individual burner may not work because it is faulty or its burner element switch is faulty. Examine the terminals of the burner element for damage. If the terminals are lightly corroded, clean them with fine steel wool. If the terminals are burned or badly pitted, replace the burner element. Test the burner element by plugging it into a receptacle that works. If it works there, check the switch. If it doesn't work, replace the burner element.

Switches are usually located on a console above the range. For access, unplug the range and pull it away from the wall. Remove the screws from the back panel and take off the panel. Check the switch for loose wires or obvious damage. The power-supply wires are attached to the switch on terminals marked "L1" and "L2." The wires from the switch to the burner element are connected to terminals marked "H1" and "H2," or just "1" and "2."

Turn a working switch on to the position that does not work on the faulty element. Using a multitester, test each power-supply terminal against each burner terminal and record or remember the results. Then try the same test with the switch on the faulty burner element. If the results are not the same, replace the switch.

Inoperative Oven or Broiler: If the oven or the broiler does not heat, first check to see if the timer is set correctly. Next, test the heating element. The oven and broiler heating elements operate in the same way. Unplug the oven and open or remove the door. Remove the nuts or screws that fasten the heating element to the back of the oven. Pull the element forward to expose its wiring, label the terminals, and disconnect the wiring.

Set a multitester at RX1 and touch the probes to the terminals of the heating element. There should be partial resistance. Next, test for ground by placing one probe on a heating-element terminal and the other probe on an insulated portion of the element. The multitester should not register any movement. If the heating element fails either of these tests, it is defective, and it should be replaced with an identical part.

Self-Cleaning: If the self-cleaning cycle will not start, first check to see that the door lock is engaged and that the timers are properly set. Self-cleaning ovens generally have two timers, one for the starting time and one for the completion time. Unless you want to delay the self-cleaning cycle, leave the starting timer at the present setting. Set the completion timer to two to three hours later than the start time. Lock the oven door and turn the oven controls to the cleaning settings. If the oven appears to go through the cleaning cycle but the oven is not clean afterward, check the baking and broiling elements as discussed above.

Cooking: If the oven doesn't appear to be holding the correct temperature, if food is overcooked or undercooked, there are several possibilities that need to be examined. First, check the temperature of the oven with an oven thermometer. Put the thermometer on a shelf in the center of the oven and set the oven for 350 degrees. Check the thermometer after 20 minutes, and then three more times every 10 minutes afterward. Add the four readings and divide by four. If the average reading is off by 25 to 50 degrees, the temperature control should be recalibrated. If the average is off by more than 50 degrees (that is, if the average is less than 300 degrees or more than 400 degrees), then the temperature control should be replaced.

To calibrate the oven temperature control, pull the temperature control knob off the control panel. Some models have a ring on the back of the knob with marks indicating "RAISE" or "LOWER." If so, turn the knob to move the ring to a higher or lower setting, depending on the results of your test. (You may have to loosen two set screws on the back of the knob first. Tighten them again after resetting the knob.)

If you do not see these marks on the back of the knobs, then the calibration is done on the control panel of the range itself. With the power off, loosen the screws on the side of the temperature control shaft. Turn the shaft one-eighth of a turn to the right to lower the temperature, or to the left to raise it.

After recalibrating the temperature control, check the temperature again with an oven thermometer. If the temperature is still wrong, check the temperature control, and replace it if necessary.

The temperature control is on the back side of the control

panel, behind the oven temperature control knob. Examine the control, and replace it if any of the wiring terminals are burned or badly discolored. Next, test the control for continuity. If it has two terminals, test the control with a continuity tester. If there are more than two terminals, check the wiring diagram on the rear panel for the pair of terminals to test. With one wire of the pair disconnected, connect the probes to the terminals and set the oven temperature control to 300 degrees. If the tester does not indicate continuity, replace the control. To replace the temperature control, you will first have to remove the capillary tube from the oven.

The capillary tube is the sensor that monitors the temperature. This tube is usually mounted on the upper left wall of the oven. As a general rule, it should not be cleaned or even touched. Check to see that this tube is not bent or broken, and that it is not touching the oven wall. In self-cleaning ovens, the capillary tube contains extremely caustic material. When examining or attempting to straighten this tube, wear rubber gloves.

To remove the capillary tube, unclip it from its supports and push it through the hole in the rear of the oven. There may be a cover or baffle over the hole, secured by a screw. Take particular care to avoid bending the tube. Pull the tube through from the back of the oven.

Next unscrew the temperature control screws on the front of the control panel and remove the oven temperature control from the back of the panel. Label the wires and disconnect them from the control. Install a new control by reversing the steps listed above. Make sure that the calibration ring is centered before replacing the temperature control knob on the control panel.

GAS RANGES

Gas ranges have very few moving parts to break or malfunction, and most of the options or accessories are electrical. Gas ranges fall into two major categories: those that have gas pilot lights and those with electrical igniters. Most problems with gas ranges can be avoided by proper maintenance and cleaning. Malfunctions are usually caused by dirt and food spills clogging burners and air shutters.

In general, any repairs to the gas-supply line should be left to professionals. If the connection between the gas-supply line and the range is a rigid connection, do not move the gas range. Have a gas-company technician disconnect the gas before moving the appliance. If the gas-supply line connection is a flexible tube, you may carefully move the range for cleaning or access.

Natural gas has no odor, but utility companies mix in an additive that gives gas its distinctive smell. If you smell gas around your gas range, check to see if the pilot light is lit. If the smell is very strong, ventilate the room as much as possible and call your gas company for service.

If the pilot light is out, make sure that all controls are turned to off, ventilate the room, and lift and prop up the range top. There is a pilot light on each side of the range, midway between the burners on each side. Light a match and hold it near the pilot-light opening.

If the pilot light does not stay lit, clean the opening carefully with a toothpick. If the pilot-light opening has a protective covering, resembling a small metal tent, remove it by pressing it on the tabs on each side. Clean the pilot-light opening and replace the protective covering.

If the pilot light still will not stay lit, it probably needs to be adjusted. The adjustment screw is either on the side of the pilot light or on the pilot gas line near the front of the range. The pilot-light flame should be a small blue cone, about a quarter inch high. Use a small screwdriver to turn the pilot light adjustment screws clockwise to increase the flame height or counterclockwise to decrease it.

Many modern gas ranges have electric igniters. If a burner won't light, raise the top of the stove and observe the igniter when you turn on the burner. If the igniter does not spark, turn on the other burner on the same side of the range. If that burner lights, then the burner control on the first burner is faulty and should be serviced by a professional.

If the electric igniter does not spark for either burner, unscrew and remove the bracket over the igniter. Clean the igniter, checking it for damage, and replace it if it is burned or cracked. To replace the igniter, unplug the range and trace the cable from the igniter to the ignition control module, a box mounted on the back of the range. (Do not move the range if it has a rigid pipe gas-supply line.) Unscrew and remove the cover on the module box and unplug the cable to the faulty igniter.

Unscrew the bracket over the igniter and remove any clips holding the igniter to the burner support. Tie a piece of string to the igniter cable where you disconnected it from the ignition control module. Pull the igniter cable out through the hole in the top of the range, pulling the string along with it. Untie the string, tie it to the end of the cable of the replacement igniter, and pull the string back to thread the new cable back to the ignition control module.

If none of the igniters work, the problem is with the ignition control module. With the range unplugged, label all the wires leading to the module, disconnect the wires, and unscrew and remove the module. Replace the module with a new part and reassemble.

If the oven fails to light, check the oven pilot light or

igniter. Open the oven door and the broiler door and wait 5 to 10 minutes for any gas to dissipate. If the oven burner is accessible from below, light a match and hold it at the tip of the pilot light, which is located at the rear of the oven burner assembly. Some ovens have a safety button that must be held in while lighting the pilot. If the burner assembly is not accessible from underneath, you will have to remove the oven bottom by lifting it directly out (there may be small locking tabs that have to be moved forward first). Next remove the baffle under the oven bottom to gain access to the burner assembly.

If the oven will not light even though the pilot is lit, the pilot flame may be set too low. Check to see if there is a pilot adjustment screw on the safety valve at the rear of the burner assembly. Turn the adjustment screw counterclockwise very slightly until the pilot flame is about a quarter inch high. If the oven will still not light, call for professional service.

If there is not a pilot adjustment screw on the safety valve at the rear of the oven burner assembly, pull the dial off the oven temperature control knob. Check for a slotted adjustment screw behind the knob, sometimes marked "P" or "Pilot." If the adjustment screw is not here, raise the cooktop and look for the screw on the back of the thermostat. Turn the pilot adjustment screw counterclockwise in very small increments until the pilot flame is about a quarter inch high. If the oven will still not light, call for professional service.

If the oven has an electric igniter, unplug the range and unscrew the igniter mounting bracket. Remove the igniter and inspect it for cracks or damage. Replace the igniter with an identical part if it is damaged in any way. To replace the igniter, trace its cable to the ignition control module on the back of the range. Disconnect the cable and tie a string to the end of the cable. Pull the igniter cable out through the oven, tie the string on the end of the new cable, and use the string to pull the cable back to the ignition control module.

GARBAGE DISPOSERS

A garbage disposer is a machine built into the kitchen sink drain that grinds garbage into pieces small enough to be rinsed down the drain. There are two basic types of garbage disposers, the continuous-feed model and the batch-feed model. The continuous-feed model is the most common. It is controlled by a wall switch and garbage can be dumped into it while it is running. The batch-feed model is operated by inserting a stopper in the sink drain and turning it to activate the garbage disposer.

In either model, a spinning flywheel attached to the motor shaft then grinds the garbage between the shredder ring and the impellers. The shredder ring is a collarlike device surrounding the area above the flywheel. The impellers are sturdy metal blocks mounted on the flywheel.

Proper use of the garbage disposer will avoid most problems. Read the manufacturer's instructions, and be careful as to what you put down the disposer. Metal, plastic, rubber, and cloth can damage the garbage disposer. Such waste as corn husks or artichoke leaves can clog the mechanism and overheat the motor. Always keep the cold water running while operating the garbage disposer, and feed garbage in slowly so as to avoid overworking the machine.

Do not use chemical drain cleaners on garbage disposers. These chemicals can damage plastic or rubber parts. To avoid odors, do not let garbage stand in the disposer for any length of time, and grind up some orange or lemon rinds occasionally to clean out old odors.

If the disposer does not work at all, check fuses or circuit breakers to see that there is power to the disposer. If the disposer quits in the middle of its operation, particularly if you were disposing tough, fibrous waste such as corn husks or carrot peelings, the flywheel is probably jammed. This situation is usually accompanied by poor water drainage, if not a complete blockage.

Start by shutting off power to the garbage disposer. Many garbage disposers have a power cord that is plugged into a standard electrical outlet under the sink. In this case, simply unplug the cord. A jammed disposer will tip the built-in overload protector. Reach into the disposer from the top and try to find a piece of silverware or some other object that jammed the flywheel. If there is an obstruction, remove it, push the overload-protector reset button, and restore power. Allow the motor time to cool if it has overheated, and turn on the disposer.

If the disposer is still jammed, disconnect the power and free the flywheel. Some garbage disposers have a factory-supplied hex wrench that fits into the bottom of the disposer. Turn the wrench back and forth to free the mechanism. If there is not a hex opening on the bottom of the disposer, stick a broom handle into the drain, wedge it against one of the impellers on the flywheel, and rotate the mechanism. Push the overload-protector reset button, allow the motor to cool, restore power, and try the disposer.

If the garbage disposer jams because of being clogged by tough waste, the drain is probably blocked also. The drain from the garbage disposer is connected to the regular household drain. The connection, particularly in more modern houses, is usually made with plastic pipe fittings that can be disassembled by hand. The clog usually occurs in the U-shaped or J-shaped trap, backing up into the garbage disposer.

Bail any standing water out of the sink. Clear out a

space under the sink to allow you to place a small pail or a large pan under the trap. Unscrew the connectors and remove the trap. Remove any debris from inside the trap or from connecting pipes. Reassemble the parts and run water to test for leaks.

If the flywheel was not jammed, or if you have removed the jam and the disposer still does not work, check the switch to see if it is faulty. For a wall switch, turn off power at the main service panel and remove the switch. If the switch is broken or the toggle is loose, replace the switch. With the switch in the on position, connect a continuity tester to the two terminals. If the tester does not indicate continuity, replace the switch. If the disposer still does not work, have a professional service the motor.

DISHWASHERS

More modern homes have built-in dishwashers. The dishwasher works by filling its tub (the bottom of the dishwasher) with water and releasing dishwasher detergent from the dispenser on the door. The heating element in the bottom of the tub heats the water, and the heated soapy water is pumped through the spray tower and the spinning spray arm to clean the dishes. The dishes are then rinsed, the dishwasher drains, and the heating element warms the air inside the dishwasher, drying the dishes.

Built-in dishwashers have permanent electrical and plumbing connections. Portable dishwashers operate in the same manner, but must be plugged in to a wall socket and have hoses attached to the sink.

Incomplete Cleaning: The most common problem with dishwashers is that the dishes are still dirty after running the machine. There are many possible causes of this problem. The first thing to check is that the dishes are loaded properly. Read the manufacturer's loading directions, making sure that dishes do not block the top opening of the spray tower (the column or cone that stands upright in the middle of the dishwasher) and that dishes do not prevent the spray arm or arms from spinning freely. Also make sure that the dishes are not loaded in such a manner as to prevent water from getting in between the dishes.

Check the dishwashing-detergent dispenser on the inside of the door to see that the dispenser is operating correctly and that the detergent is being released during the wash cycle. Improper loading may have resulted in a dish or pan resting against the door and preventing it from opening. If this happens repeatedly, check the dispenser for faulty parts.

The detergent-dispenser door is opened mechanically by the dishwasher timer during the wash cycle. Turn off the power to the dishwasher and check the dispenser for caked-on detergent or other debris that might keep the door from operating properly. Clean the dispenser and any moving parts. Remove the door panel by loosening the retaining screws around the inside of the dishwasher door. You may have to lift a metal strip to gain access to the retaining screws. Check the detergent-dispensing mechanism on the inside of the door, making sure that nothing is stuck or broken. Replace any broken parts and reassemble the door.

Cleaning may be incomplete because the water is not hot enough. Start the dishwasher and open the door during the first wash cycle. There will be water standing in the bottom of the dishwasher. Test the water with a thermometer. It should be at least 140 degrees. If it is not, try turning up the temperature setting on your water heater.

If that does not take care of the problem, test the heating element to see that it is functioning properly. Turn off the power to the dishwasher and remove the access panel on the front of the machine by removing any retaining screws and pulling off the panel. Disconnect the heating-element terminal wires under the tub. Set a multitester to RX1 and attach the probes to the heating-element terminals. The meter should indicate partial resistance. If not, the heating element is faulty and should be replaced.

If the meter indicates partial resistance, check for ground. There are rubber covers on the heating elements between the tub and the terminals. Pull one of these rubber covers down far enough to expose the metal underneath. Touch one probe of the multitester to this metal and the other probe to the other terminal. If the meter indicates any continuity, the heating element is faulty and should be replaced.

To replace the heating element, slide off both rubber covers under the tub and remove the locknuts that were under the rubber covers. From inside the dishwasher, lift out the old heating element and replace it with an identical part. Replace the locknuts, rubber washers, and wires under the tub.

Incomplete cleaning can also be caused by low water pressure. Avoid this problem by not turning on the water in other parts of the house while the dishwasher is running. To check this, start the dishwasher and open the door toward the end of the wash cycle. (Keep your face away from the door until the steam in the dishwasher is fully released.) Allow the water to cool and bail it out of the dishwasher tub using a cup or some other container, removing the rotating spray arm if necessary. Measure the amount of water you remove. If it is less than 2½ gallons, you have a problem with low water pressure.

Leaks: Water can leak from under the dishwasher or from around the door. Leaks around the door can be caused by the use of the wrong detergent or by improperly loaded dishes deflecting water through the door vent. Make sure that you use only dishwasher detergent, and that dishes are not prewashed and loaded with soap left on them. If the dishwasher continues to leak around the door, either the door is not closing tightly or the door gasket is defective.

Check to see that the door is closed tightly when the door catch is engaged. If not, the door catch can be adjusted by loosening the retaining screws and sliding the catch. If the door gasket is hardened or damaged, it should be replaced. The gasket may be held in place by clips or tabs that can be pried out, or it may be held by retaining screws. Soak the new gasket in warm water if necessary to make it pliable. If the gasket fits into a track or groove, lubricate the gasket with soapy water to make installation easier. Some models may have an additional gasket on the tub. Examine this and replace if necessary.

Leaks under the tub may be caused by loose hose connections. Remove the access panel on the front of the dishwasher and examine the drain hose and water-inlet hose connections under the tub. Tighten any loose connections, replacing any leaking hoses or faulty clamps.

Leaks can also be caused by a cracked tub or by a faulty pump seal. A visible crack in the tub can be sealed with epoxy glue or with silicone rubber sealant. A faulty pump seal requires professional service.

Excessive Noise: Noise may be caused by improperly loaded dishes knocking against each other or being hit by a spinning spray arm. Noise while the dishwasher is filling with water can be caused by low water pressure. Check the water pressure as discussed above and if necessary avoid running water in other parts of the house while the dishwasher is operating.

Excessive noise may also be caused by a clogged water-inlet valve screen or by a faulty water-inlet valve. The water-inlet valve is accessible through the front access panel. The water-inlet line is attached to it, with a hose leading to the dishwasher tub. With the power and the water turned off, remove the wires from the inlet-valve solenoid terminals. Set a multitester to RX1 and test for continuity. If there is no continuity, replace the valve.

To replace the water-inlet valve, or to clean the filter screen, place a small pan or other container under the valve and remove the hose and waterline connections. Remove any screws holding the valve to the tub. Pry out the water-inlet valve screen. If it is plastic, clean it well; if it is metal replace it. Reinstall the valve and reconnect the waterline, the tub hose, and the wires.

Dishwasher Does Not Run: If the dishwasher will not run, check to see if the circuit breaker is tripped or the fuse is blown. If there is power to the dishwasher, the door switch may be faulty. To check the door switch, first make sure that the door closes properly. The door catch can be adjusted by loosening the retaining screws, moving the catch, and retightening the screws.

If the door catch is working properly, turn off the power and remove the control panel. This is the upper portion of the door that holds any switches or dials controlling the dishwasher. Remove the control panel by loosening the retaining screws located inside the dishwasher door. Be sure to hold the control panel to keep it from falling. Close the dishwasher door and lower the control panel for access to the door switch.

Disconnect the wires from the door-switch terminals, set a multitester to RX1, and touch the probes to the terminals. If the tester indicates no continuity, the door switch is faulty and should be replaced. Open the door, remove the door-switch retaining screws in the top of the door, and replace the switch.

If the door switch is operating properly, the timer may be faulty. The timer is also located in the door behind the control panel. With the power off and the control panel removed, disconnect the timer motor wires and connect a multitester to the terminals. With the multitester set at RX100, the meter should indicate partial resistance. If not, the motor is faulty and the timer should be replaced. If the motor is okay, work the timer plug off the timer and inspect it for loose contacts or other damage.

Check the timer terminals by referring to the wiring diagram on the inside of the door panel. Identify the pairs of terminals controlling each cycle and test for continuity with a multitester set at RX1 with the dial set at the proper setting according to the chart on the diagram. If any pair of terminals are faulty, replace the timer.

To replace the timer, pull off the timer dial and remove the screws mounting the timer to the door. Disconnect all wires, marking them as you do so. Install a new timer, reconnect the wires, and install the timer plug. Replace the dial and put the control panel back on the front of the machine.

WASHING MACHINES

The home clothes washer consists of three primary systems that function together to clean the clothes. The plumbing system brings water into the machine, circulates it, and drains it back out again. The mechanical system provides the cleaning action of the tub and the agitator, and the electrical system powers and controls the entire process. A problem can usually be initially diagnosed as arising from a particular system, and then tracked down from there.

Washer Won't Run: If the washer does not run at all, start by checking that there is power to the machine. If the washer quit while running, the motor may have overheated, particularly if it was operating with a very heavy load (such as rugs) or if it had been used for many loads. Allow the motor to cool for an hour or more and retry it.

If the washer simply will not start, first examine the lid switch. Many washers have a safety switch that does not allow the machine to operate if the lid is open. Raise the top of the washer, either by removing the retaining screws under the lid or by releasing the spring catches at the front by sliding a putty knife into the slot between the top and the main body of the washer and pushing on the catches. The lid switch is attached to the underside of the top of the washer. Disconnect the wires and attach the probes of a continuity tester to the terminals of the switch. The tester should indicate continuity when the switch lever is raised, and should not indicate continuity with the lever lowered. If the switch fails either test, it should be replaced.

If the lid switch is not faulty, check the timer. The timer controls the starting, stopping, and various cycles of the washer. The timer dial is the main control that starts the machine. With the power off, remove the control panel, the panel with the control dials and switches. The retaining screws holding the control panel in place may be hidden by an adhesive strip across the bottom of the control console, or they may be on the top or the back of the console.

Check the wiring diagram (in the owner's manual) for the terminals that control different wash cycles. If a particular cycle is not working properly, check the appropriate terminals. Otherwise check all the terminals. Set a multitester to RX1 and see that the terminals indicate continuity. If not, replace the timer. To test the timer motor, located under the timer cover, disconnect the wires from the motor terminals, set a multitester to RX100, and attach the probes to the terminals. The tester should indicate resistance of 2000 to 3000 ohms. If not, replace the motor.

Washer Won't Fill: If the washer appears to start but

there is no water running into the tub, start by checking that the faucets are turned on. Also, inspect the hoses running from the faucets to the washer to see that they are not kinked or bent. Next, inspect the filter screens to see that they are not clogged. With the power and the water turned off, disconnect the water hoses at both ends. Put a bucket under each hose end as you disconnect it. Inspect the filter screens at the inlet-valve ports (where the hoses attach to the washer) to see that they are not rusted or blocked. Clean the screens or replace them if necessary.

Next, check the water-inlet valve. Raise the top of the washer and remove the splash guard if there is one. The water-inlet valve is located in the left rear corner of the machine, either on the back of the cabinet behind the tub or mounted on a corner bracket. If the valve is mounted on the cabinet, label and remove the wires from one solenoid. With a multitester set to RX100, connect tester probes to the terminals. The tester should indicate resistance of 500 to 2000 ohms. Repeat the test on the other solenoid. If either solenoid fails to register the proper resistance, replace the unit.

If the water-inlet valve is mounted on the underside of a corner bracket, remove the screws holding it to the bracket and push the valve down so that it is accessible through the back of the washer. Label and disconnect the wires and set a multitester at RX100. Attach the probes to the terminals of a solenoid. The tester should indicate some resistance. Repeat the test on the other solenoid. If either solenoid is faulty, replace the unit.

Water Leaks: The first step is to check all water hoses to see that they are on tightly. The drain hose is usually held on with a spring-type clamp that can work loose over time from vibration. Inspect the hoses for cracks or other damage. Inspect interior hoses and connections for leaks at the same time.

If the washer still leaks, and if the leak is not excessive, try to locate the leak while running the water. If the water pump is leaking, it will have to be replaced. Unplug the washer and turn off the water and disconnect the hoses. Have a bucket ready to catch any water left in the hoses or in the pump. There are two basic clothes-washer designs. Type-I washers have the water pump accessible from the bottom. Type-II washers have the pump accessible from the back.

For a Type-I washer, lay the machine down on a tarp or some other material to protect the finish (and if necessary the floor). The pump will have two or more hoses attached. Remove the hose clamps and pull the hoses off the pump ports. Remove the pump mounting bolts using a socket wrench. Observe how the pump control lever fits into its slot, so that you can install the new pump correctly.

For a Type-II washer, unplug the washer, turn off the water, and disconnect the hoses. Remove the rear access panel and have a bucket ready to catch any water. The pump is mounted on the bottom of the tub, and has several hoses connected to it. The pump coupling is below the pump, and is secured to it by a circular clamp. Unscrew the clamp and remove the pump coupling from the pump. Remove the screws or bolts that hold the pump to the underside of the tub and pull the pump free. Remove the hose clamps and remove the hoses from the pump. Inspect the pump for damage or cracks. If there is any damage or if the pump was leaking, replace it.

No Agitation Action: If the clothes washer seems to operate through the full cycle but the clothes are not getting clean, the washer may not be agitating properly. Observe the beginning of the wash cycle with the lid up to see if the agitator is working properly.

With the washer unplugged, remove the agitator and inspect it for wear or damage. On a Type-I washer, unscrew the plastic cap on the top of the agitator and then unscrew the stud inside the agitator with a wrench. If the top of the agitator does not unscrew easily, then there is a lid on the top that is pried off to gain access to a nut underneath. Lift the agitator straight up, tapping it lightly to free it if it is stuck on the shaft.

On a Type-II washer, the agitator should pull right off when tugged on both sides of the base. If the agitator sticks, tap it sharply to free it. As an alternative, pry the cap off the top of the agitator and put a few drops of oil on the shaft.

Inspect the agitator for damage, checking for wear on the gear teeth on the inside of the agitator. If the teeth are worn smooth, or if the agitator is cracked, replace it.

If the agitator is in good shape, check to see that the drive belt is not worn or loose. Unplug the washer and turn off the water supply. Remove the back panel and check the drive belt. Push down on the belt with your thumb. If the belt can be depressed more than a half inch, it is too loose. A Type-I washer has the motor mounted on a bracket toward the back of the cabinet, to the side of the pump. Loosen the motor bracket enough to be able to move the motor slightly. Tap the right side of the motor with a hammer, moving the motor enough to tighten the belt. When the drive belt feels tight enough, retighten the nut holding the motor bracket. If the belt appears to be worn, it should be replaced.

A Type-II washer has the motor mounted on a mounting plate, directly below the pump. To adjust the belt, loosen the motor mounting nuts, pull the motor toward you, and retighten the nuts. If the belt is worn, replace it. Unscrew the clamps above and below the pump coupling and remove the coupling. Loosen the motor mounting nuts and turn the transmission pulley as you pry the belt off. Remove the belt from the clutch pulley above the motor and pull it out of the washer.

The washer may fail to agitate properly because of a faulty lid switch or, on a Type-I washer, a faulty wigwag. Testing and replacing the lid switch was discussed above. The wigwag is a set of solenoids that controls the agitation and spin of the machine. The wigwag is located on top of the transmission. There are two solenoids, each with a pair of wires connected to it. To test the solenoids, unplug the washer and set a multitester to RX10. Remove the wires from the terminals and touch a probe to each terminal. The multitester should indicate 200 to 700 ohms. Repeat the test on the other solenoid. If either solenoid fails the test, replace the wigwag.

No Spinning Action: If the washer does not spin properly, the problem is usually one of the same causes listed above for not agitating. Check the lid switch, the wigwag, and the drive belt to see that they are operating correctly.

Excessive Noise: If the washer is making excessive noise and vibrating badly, first check that the load is balanced and that the washer is level. Level the washer by adjusting the leveling feet that screw in and out of the bottom of the cabinet.

Excessive noise may also be caused by a slipping drive belt or by loose transmission braces. Check the belt for looseness, and tighten it if necessary as discussed above. Check the transmission mounting braces, and make sure that all nuts and bolts are tight.

CLOTHES DRYERS

A clothes dryer is a relatively simple machine, consisting of a motor, a heating element, and an air blower. The motor turns the drum to tumble the clothes. The blower forces air past the gas or electric heater and into the drum. Controls can include switches, timers, and thermostats. Many problems can be avoided by simple maintenance. Lint is a major cause of dryer problems. Clean the lint filter after every load, and clean out the exhaust vent periodically.

If the dryer will not operate at all, first check that it has power. Remember that electric dryers operate on 240-volt circuits, and thus have two circuit breakers in the main service panel. Next, check to see that the door switch is operating correctly. The door switch is a safety device that prevents the dryer from operating when the door is open. Unplug the dryer and raise the top. Some dryers (those with a top-mounted lint screen) have two screws at the front of the lint screen slot that have to be removed first. Then release the hidden top clips by inserting a putty knife under the top and pushing in on the clips.

The door switch is mounted inside the cabinet above the door. Disconnect the wires and touch the probes of a continuity tester to the terminals. The tester should indicate continuity when the door is closed, and no continuity when the door is opened. If the switch is faulty, replace it with an identical part.

The dryer may also fail to operate because of a faulty start switch or a faulty timer. With the dryer unplugged, release the back of the control console and tilt it forward. Label the wires going to the start switch and disconnect them. For a two-terminal switch, attach the probes of a continuity tester to the two terminals. The tester should not indicate continuity. With the probes attached, press the starter switch. With the switch pressed, the tester should indicate continuity.

For a three-terminal switch, place one probe on the

terminal marked either "NC" or "CT1," and the other probe on the terminal marked "CO" or "R1." The tester should indicate continuity. When the start button is pushed, the tester should not indicate continuity. If the switch fails either test, replace it.

With the control console open, also test the timer. Test the timer motor by disconnecting its wires and attaching a multitester set to RX1000. The tester should indicate resistance of 2000 to 3000 ohms. Test the timer by checking the dryer's wiring diagram and finding which terminals control which cycles. Set the knob to the cycle and touch the probes to the terminals that control that cycle. The tester should indicate continuity. If the motor or the timer fail these tests, they should be replaced.

No Heat: If the motor runs but the dryer does not heat, the timer or the temperature selector switch may be faulty. Check the timer as discussed above. To check the temperature selector switch, unplug the dryer and loosen the control console. Check the dryer's wiring diagram to see which terminals on the temperature selector switch control which drying cycle. Label the wires and disconnect them. Set the control to a cycle and test the terminals that control that cycle. The tester should indicate continuity. Repeat for each cycle or setting. If the switch fails to pass any test, it should be replaced.

Lack of heat may also be caused by a faulty centrifugal switch. This switch is mounted on the motor, and may be accessible through a toe panel, a small panel on the front of the dryer cabinet at the bottom. If there is no toe panel, lift the top and remove the front panel. With the dryer unplugged, label and remove the wires and unscrew the switch from the motor. Attach the probes of a continuity tester to terminals one and two. With the switch button out, the tester should indicate continuity. With the button in, the tester should indicate resistance. Connect the probes to terminals five and six. The results should be the same. Next, connect one probe to terminal five and the other to the terminal marked either "3" OR "BK." With the switch button out, the tester should indicate resistance, and with the button in it should show continuity. If the switch fails any of these tests, it should be replaced.

Finally, failure to heat could mean that the heating element is faulty. To test the heating element, unplug the dryer and remove the rear panel. Label and disconnect the wires to the heating-element terminals. Set a multitester to RX1. For a two-terminal element, touch the probes to the two terminals. The tester should indicate 5 to 50 ohms of resistance. Next, touch one probe to the heating-element housing and the other to first one and then the other terminal. The tester needle should not move for either test.

For a three-terminal heating element, touch one probe to the middle terminal and the other probe to first one and then the other of the outer terminals. In each case, the meter should indicate 10 to 40 ohms. To test for a ground, touch one probe to the housing box and the other probe to each terminal in turn. The meter needle should not move at any of these tests. If the heating element fails any test, it is faulty and should be replaced.

Excessive Noise: First check to see that the dryer is level. If not, adjust the leveling feet that screw in and out of the cabinet. Next, check for loose parts, including cabinet panels and trim. Tighten screws or adjust clips to keep parts from vibrating.

Excessive noise may also be caused by a worn drive belt of a worn or broken idler. Check the drive belt by removing the front panel, lifting the drum slightly, and removing the belt. Inspect the belt and replace it if it is worn. At the same time, check the idler, the pulley that takes up the slack in the belt. Push the idler pulley toward the motor and slip the belt off the motor pulley. Inspect the idler for wear or damage, and replace it if necessary.

CHAPTER
6

. . . .

Electronics

The modern home has more electronic devices than ever before, for entertainment, for communication, and for information. The first thing to do when electronic equipment is not functioning correctly is to check that the equipment is hooked up properly. This is particularly likely to be the cause of malfunction when two or more components are linked together for operation. Many home electronics devices are used in connection with other pieces of equipment. A telephone is often used with an answering machine. A computer system has a central processing unit (CPU), a monitor, a keyboard, and a printer. A typical home entertainment system has a TV, a VCR, a receiver, a tape deck, a CD player, and speakers. Improper cable connections of any two pieces of equipment can result in a failure of the entire system.

TELECOMMUNICATIONS

Telecommunications equipment in the home is still usually limited to several relatively simple telephones and possibly an answering machine. Although FAX machines are becoming more and more common, if not necessary, in the business world, most homes do not have them yet.

TELEPHONES

At one time, the home telephone was supplied by the telephone company, and was permanently wired to the inside wiring system installed by the same phone company. Today, contractors install telephone wiring in new homes at the same time that they install the electrical wiring system. Telephone jacks are installed in various rooms in the same manner as electrical outlets. And telephones are plugged into the jacks just like lamps are plugged into outlets.

For most people today, this means that they own and are responsible for the maintenance and repair of their telephones and of the telephone wiring inside their homes. Some local telephone companies do offer inside wiring maintenance contracts at an additional charge. If you are paying for such a contract, it will be listed as a separate line item on your monthly telephone bill. The low monthly cost of such a contract can be deceptive, since, as you will see, problems with the telephone system in your home very rarely involve the wiring.

If your telephone does not work, unplug it and try it in another jack. If it still does not work and you have another phone in the house, try that phone. If that phone works, plug it into the jack where the first phone did not work. If the second phone works in the first wall jack, then the first phone was faulty.

If neither phone works, the problem is either with the inside wiring or with the telephone line coming to your house. On the outside of the house is a telephone line protector, the interface between the telephone company's wiring and your house wiring. The wiring from your house connects to this interface via a jack just like the ones in your house. Take a working phone and plug it into the jack inside the protector. If the phone works, there may be a problem with your inside wiring. Check the connections at the protector to see that the wiring from the house is properly connected to the protector. If the phone does not work, there is a problem with the telephone company's line coming into your house.

If you have determined that a phone is faulty, first check the line cord and the handset cord to see that all connections are plugged in properly. Inspect the cords for wear or damage. Replace the cords with cords from a working phone and see if the faulty phone works. Inspect the switch hook and the keypad to see that all parts move freely and are clean. If the phone still does not work, the problem is probably with the circuit board, and the phone should be repaired or replaced. It is generally less expensive to replace a basic telephone that to have it repaired.

ANSWERING MACHINES

If a new answering machine does not work, it is probably not connected properly. Reread the instruction manual and reconnect the power and telephone lines. If the machine has been working and now won't work, first check to see that it has power. If the machine is plugged in and the circuit breaker is not tripped, inspect the power cord for wear or damage. To test the power cord, locate the power-cord terminals inside the machine. Touch a probe of a continuity tester to one prong of the power-cord plug and the other probe to each end of the power cord. The tester should indicate continuity once, and not twice. Repeat the test with the other prong of the power-cord plug. If the power cord fails any test, replace it.

If the answering machine works but the messages are not clear, replace the audiocassette. At the same time, clean the tape transport mechanism and demagnetize the tape heads.

Use the same cleaning and demagnetizing devices used for stereo tape decks, available at stereo or electronic stores.

VIDEO

The average home has several televisions, and usually a videocassette recorder (VCR) connected to one of the TVs. Laser-disc players are starting to become popular also. A laser-disc player is essentially a large CD player. If you are having problems with a laser disc, see the section below dealing with CD players.

TELEVISIONS

Virtually all the controls and components of modern television sets are solid-state electronics, with little to go wrong and little if anything serviceable by a nonprofessional. Most problems with TVs and VCRs involve improper control settings or cable connections with other electronic components or with the antenna or cable hookup.

If the TV works but there is no picture, begin by inspecting the antenna or cable system connections. If you have an outdoor antenna, check the antenna signal cable to see that the connections are good at the TV, at the antenna, and at any connections or junctions in between.

If there is a picture, but it is distorted, the antenna may not be positioned correctly. Some outdoor antennas have a motor-driven rotor control to turn the antenna for the best picture. If you do not have a rotor control, turn the antenna by hand to obtain the best picture. If you do have a rotor control and it is not operating, first check to see that it has power. Check the power cord by locating the power-cord terminals and touching one probe of a continuity tester to a prong of the power-cord plug and the other probe to both ends of the cord. The tester should indicate continuity for one end of the power cord but not for the other. Repeat the test on the other prong of the power-cord plug. Replace the power cord if it fails any of these tests.

The power cable carries power from the rotor control in the house to the rotor on the antenna. To check the power cable, unplug the power cord in the house and gain access to the rotor, usually through a small door in the bottom of the rotor housing. The three wires of the power cable are connected to the power-cable terminal block in the rotor housing. Check the connections for loose or damaged wires. Label the power-cable wires and disconnect them from the terminal block. Touch the probe of a continuity tester to one wire and then touch the other probe to each of the other two wires. Repeat the test with all combinations of wires. The tester should not indicate any continuity. If there is continuity between any two wires, replace the power cable.

If there is no continuity, twist all three wires together and test the wires of the power cable at the rotor control in the house. This time, there should be continuity between any combination of two wires. If not, replace the power cable.

If the power cable is okay, clean and lubricate the rotor-gear assembly in the rotor housing. You may have to take down the antenna to remove the gear assembly. If the rotor will still not work, the motor is probably faulty and should be replaced.

If you have cable and there is no picture, first check to see that the cable connections are tight and that the cable converter box is plugged in. Try the controls at the converter box rather than using the remote control. If the TV works now, the remote batteries are probably dead. If the remote does not work with new batteries, the remote is faulty and should be replaced. Most modern TVs are cable ready. This means that they will work with a direct cable connection without using the converter box. Try disconnecting the cable connection from the wall outlet to the converter box and reconnecting it to the TV. If you do get a picture this way, the converter box is faulty. If it is the property of the cable company, have it repaired or replaced by them. If your TV is cable ready, you can continue to operate it with the cable connected directly to the TV. The possible downside to this is that the programming may not be on the same channels with a direct cable connection as they are when you use a converter box.

If the antenna or cable system is properly connected but the TV does not work, check to see if the remote control is working by operating the TV controls manually. If the TV works with manual controls, the remote needs new batteries or is faulty.

Modern TVs have various display lights, usually at least a power-on light and a digital channel indicator. If these lights do not come on, there is no power to the unit. Check to see that the TV is plugged in and that the circuit breaker is not tripped. With the TV unplugged, open the cabinet and find the power-cord terminals. Disconnect one wire and touch the probe of a continuity tester to one prong of the power-cord plug. Touch the other probe to the end of each wire of the power cord. One wire should show continuity and the other should not. Touch one probe to the other prong of the power-cord plug and repeat the tests. If the power cord fails any of these tests, it is faulty and should be replaced.

With the TV set still unplugged, test the power fuse. Find the fuse on the power-supply circuit board and remove it with a fuse puller. Test the fuse for continuity. If there is no continuity, replace the fuse. If there is still no power to the set, the TV should be serviced by a professional.

If there is sound but no picture, or picture but no sound, the first thing to do is to check that the controls are set correctly and that the videocassette recorder is working properly. If there is still no sound, check the TV speaker or driver to see that it is functioning properly.

With the set unplugged, remove the back panel and inspect the driver wires for looseness, wear, or damage. Disconnect the wires from the driver and set a multitester to test for resistance. Touch the probes of the multitester to the driver terminals. The meter should indicate resistance close to the ohms rating listed on the driver or in the owner's manual supplied with the TV set. If the driver does not show proper resistance, replace it. If the driver is okay and there is still no sound, have the set serviced by a professional.

VCRs

The videocassette recorder is essentially a tape recorder, operating in principle much like an audio-tape deck. The VCR is able to store video as well as sound as magnetic information on a tape. Videocassettes have a safety tab on the back of the plastic casing to prevent accidental erasure of programs. The tab is connected to the main body of the case on one side, and can be easily broken off with a screwdriver. If the tab is removed, the VCR cannot record on that videocassette. If you wish to record on a videocassette that has had its safety tab removed, put a piece of tape over the slot where the tab was.

If the VCR appears to be operating normally, but the sound or picture is of very poor quality, you may simply need to adjust the tracking or clean the heads. There is generally a knob or set of buttons labeled "Tracking" with "+" and "−" (plus and minus) indicators. Adjust this setting while the tape is running to see if the picture improves. If it has been a while since you cleaned the heads in your VCR, that may be the reason your picture is bad. Borrow, rent, or buy a head-cleaning kit and see if that clears up the problem before attempting more serious repairs.

If the VCR does not play and the display lights are not lit, the unit is not getting power. Check to see that the VCR is plugged in and that there is power to the outlet. If you are using a remote control, see if the VCR will work using manual controls on the control panel. If the VCR does work from the control panel, the remote control needs new batteries or is faulty.

If the unit still does not function, unplug it and remove the top panel. Locate the terminals for the power cord and disconnect one of the wires. Touch one probe of a continuity tester to one prong of the power-cord plug and the other probe to each wire of the other end of the power cord. The tester should indicate continuity for one wire and not for the other. Repeat the test for the other prong of the power-cord plug. If the power cord fails any of these tests, it should be replaced.

If the power cord is not faulty, check the power fuse. The fuse is on the circuit board near the power-supply components. Remove the fuse with a fuse puller and touch the probes of a continuity tester to each end of the fuse. The tester should indicate continuity. If it does not, install a new fuse, using an exact replacement. If the fuse requires frequent replacement, there is probably a problem with the power supply.

After locating the power-supply components from the top, turn the chassis over and remove the bottom panel. Unscrew and remove the transformer and its circuit board. Find the fuse contact points on the circuit board. Touch one probe of a continuity tester to a fuse contact point and the other probe to a power-block contact point next to it. If there is not continuity, have the VCR serviced by a professional.

If the display lights work but there is no sound or picture, first make sure that the videocassette in the machine is not faulty and that the VCR is properly connected to the TV and that all controls are set properly. Next, check the tape transport system to make sure that it is functioning properly.

With the VCR unplugged, remove the bottom panel and inspect the drive belts. Replace any worn or damaged belts. Also replace any belt that is very loose. Clean the belts with a swab and rubber cleaner. Avoid touching the belts with your fingers.

Remove the top panel and remove the videocassette plate that covers the tape transport path. Inspect the pinch roller for flatness or damage, replacing it if necessary. To remove the pinch roller, loosen the retaining screw in the center of the roller and pull the roller straight up off the shaft. Replace the pinch roller with an identical part and reassemble the machine.

If there is a picture but no sound, or if there is sound but no picture, first make sure that the TV is operating properly, that all connections are right, and that all VCR and TV controls are set correctly. If there is still a problem, the VCR should be serviced by a professional.

If the videocassette is not loading or unloading properly, clean and lubricate the loading assembly. With the unit unplugged, remove the top panel and the front panel. Remove any obstructions or debris. Remove any dirt from the loading-assembly gears with a toothpick, and clean the gears with a swab dipped in denatured alcohol. Lubricate the gears with a toothpick and white grease, wiping off any excess grease with a clean swab.

To remove a jammed cassette, unplug the VCR and remove the top panel. Try to remove the jammed videocassette by hand, taking care not to exert too much force. It may be necessary to cut the tape to untangle it from the rollers, allowing the cassette to be pulled out through the loading door. If the cassette is still jammed in place, remove the videocassette plate, lift out the cassette, and reassemble the VCR.

STEREOS

A typical stereo system consists of a receiver (a combination radio tuner and amplifier), speakers, and one or more music reproduction devices, including a tape deck, a turntable, and a CD player. Two or more of these components may be packaged together. A "boom box," for example, has speakers, receiver, and a tape deck in a single housing, but the principles are the same as if the components were separate.

Follow directions carefully in assembling and connecting stereo components. Make sure that the speakers are wired in phase. The speaker-wire terminals on the receiver are marked "+" and "−." The terminals on the speakers themselves are also marked. They may also be marked "+" and "−" or one terminal on each speaker may be marked with the resistance in ohms.

The important thing is that the wires from the "+" terminals on the receiver must be attached to similarly marked terminals on the speakers. Speaker cable consists of two wires, usually encased in clear or semiclear insulation. The two wires are identifiably different. Either the wires themselves are made of different-colored metal (one brass, the other silver), or the insulation on one wire will have some kind of marking or striping while the insulation on the other wire is not marked. Pick a system that you can remember, such as putting the brass or marked wire on the "+" terminal, and stick with it.

Generally, all the components are wired through the

receiver, which amplifies the signal and sends it to the speakers. If a tape deck or CD player does not work, first check to see that it is properly connected to the receiver and that the receiver is working properly.

RECEIVERS

If the receiver does not work and there are no display lights working, check to see that there is power to the receiver and that the remote control, if you are using one, is working properly. See that the receiver is plugged in, that the circuit breaker is not tripped, and check to see if the receiver will turn on with the power switch on the front of the control panel.

If there are still no operating display lights, unplug the receiver and remove the top panel. Locate the terminals for the power cord and disconnect one of the wires. Touch one probe of a continuity tester to one prong of the power-cord plug and the other probe to each wire of the other end of the power cord. The tester should indicate continuity for one wire and not for the other. Repeat the test for the other prong of the power-cord plug. If the power cord fails any of these tests, it should be replaced.

If the display lights are on but there is no sound, check to see that the controls for the radio or other devices are set correctly. If there is no sound from one source but there is from another, the problem is in the source, whether a tape deck or CD player or turntable. If there is no sound from any source, including the radio, take the receiver for professional service.

If there is intermittent sound from the radio, make sure that the tuner control is properly adjusted and that the antenna, either external or built-in, is positioned properly. Also make sure that the speakers are wired properly. If the problem is only with the radio, unplug the receiver and remove the top panel. The tuner control (station-selector dial) on the front of the panel turns the variable capacitor inside the receiver. Clean the blades of the variable capacitor with compressed air or use a small amount of electronic contact cleaner. Remove any large particles of dust with a toothpick or a tissue. If the problem persists, have the receiver serviced by a professional.

TAPE DECKS

Most tape decks sold today play standard audiocassettes. The most common problems in sound quality arise from failure to properly clean the tape drive mechanism and failure to demagnetize the tape heads. Most music or equipment dealers sell cleaning kits and demagnetizers. The cleaning kit consists of a special cassette, containing cleaning material instead of recording tape, and a bottle of cleaning fluid. Follow the directions on the package to clean the tape deck. A common style of demagnetizer also looks like a cassette. It loads into the tape deck just like a tape, and electronically demagnetizes the tape heads in a second or two.

If the tape deck does not work and none of the display lights light up, check to see that the machine is plugged in and that a circuit breaker has not been tripped. Next, unplug the machine and remove the back panel. Locate the terminals for the power cord and disconnect one of the wires. Touch one probe of a continuity tester to one prong of the power-cord plug and the other probe to each wire of the other end of the power cord. The tester should indicate continuity for one wire and not for the other. Repeat the test for the other prong of the power-cord plug. If the power cord fails any of these tests, it should be replaced.

If there is still no power, test the on/off switch to see if it is functioning properly. With the unit unplugged, remove the top panel. Disconnect the control lever from the front panel to the on/off switch and unscrew the on/off switch and its circuit board from the chassis. Turn the circuit board over and touch the probes of a continuity tester to the switch pins, first with the switch in the on position and then in the off position. The tester should indicate continuity when the switch is on, and should indicate no continuity when the switch is off. If not, the switch is faulty and should be replaced. If the switch is okay and the tape deck still does not work, take it to a professional for service.

If the sound is distorted, first try the other components of the stereo system, such as the CD player or the radio. If the sound from all sources is distorted, the problem is not with the tape recorder, but with the receiver or the speakers. If the tape recorder is the only source producing distorted sound, start by cleaning and demagnetizing the tape deck as discussed above.

Next, examine the drive belt to see if it is loose or dirty. With the tape deck unplugged, remove the top panel. Inspect the drive belts for wear or damage. If a belt appears to be dirty or sticky, clean it with a swab dipped in rubber cleaner. Avoid touching the drive belts directly with your fingers. If any belts appear to be excessively loose, replace them with exact duplicate parts. To remove a belt, hold it with a pair of needle-nose pliers and slide it off its pulley.

If the sound distortion appears to be caused by the tape being played too fast or too slow, the playback speed can be adjusted on some tape decks. With the unit unplugged, remove the top panel and locate the capstan motor. All drive belts are turned by this motor. See if there is a small opening in the motor housing, with an adjustment screw inside the opening. If not, speed adjustment requires professional service.

If there is a speed adjustment screw, plug in the tape

recorder and play the tape deck for 5 to 10 minutes to warm up the motor. When adjusting the speed, it is best to play a tape with voice passages, preferably in the middle of the tape. Play the tape and turn the speed-adjustment screw back and forth slowly until the sound is at its best. Unplug the power cord and reassemble the unit.

Distorted sound can also be caused by a faulty pinch roller. With the tape deck unplugged, remove the loading door. Locate the pinch-roller assembly. The pinch roller is next to the tape heads, and the assembly pushes the roller up to push the tape against the tape drive shaft. Using a small screwdriver, pry the lock washer off the shaft and slide the pinch-roller assembly off the shaft. Examine the spring mounted on the shaft behind the pinch-roller assembly. Replace it if it is damaged. If the pinch roller is damaged or flattened, replace the assembly with an identical part.

COMPACT DISC PLAYERS

The recording industry has gradually shifted its output from vinyl records to compact discs. Most new albums are not even released on vinyl anymore, and more and more homes now have CD players as an integral part of the stereo system.

Music is encoded on a CD via a digital code stamped onto the disc. The CD player focuses a laser beam onto the tracks on the spinning disc, and the light reflected by the coding is read by an optical pickup and transformed into electrical signals. These signals are converted into a form compatible with a standard stereo receiver, and sent to the receiver, which then amplifies the signals and sends them to the speakers.

The laser beam must focus on a narrow track of code on a disc spinning at a very high rate of speed. It is relatively easy for the laser to get out of alignment. This problem often shows up as the music skipping from one part of a song to another, much like a record player skipping across grooves, but without the scratching sound of the needle. This skipping generally occurs in the first two or three songs on a CD. Realignment of the laser may have to be done every few years, and requires professional service.

The skipping may be caused by dirt on the laser lens. You might be able to see the lens by looking into the drawer where the CD goes in. If so, use a can of compressed air to blast dirt off the lens. Even if you can't see the lens, blast some air into the opening and you may solve the problem. For more advanced techniques, see below.

If the skipping problem only occurs on certain CDs, it may be that the CD surface is dirty; check the side of the CD with no printing on it, looking for dirt or heavy fingerprints. To clean a compact disc, hold the disk by the edges and wipe with a soft, dry, lint-free cloth. Wipe radially (in a straight line from the center hole outward to the edge), avoiding any circular motions. For particularly dirty or sticky discs, use a commercial CD cleaner. If the distortion persists, try another CD.

If the CD player does not work and there are no display lights, the unit is not getting power. Remove any CD in the player and unplug the unit. Remove the top panel to gain access to the power supply. Locate the terminals for the power cord and disconnect one of the wires. Touch one probe of a continuity tester to one prong of the power-cord plug and the other probe to each wire of the other end of the power cord. The tester should indicate continuity for one wire and not for the other. Repeat the test for the other prong of the power-cord plug. If the power cord fails any of these tests, it should be replaced.

If there is still no power, test the on/off switch to see if it is functioning properly. With the player unplugged, remove the top and front panels, as well as the loading platform. With the loading drawer in the out position, unscrew the loading-drawer guard and pull the loading drawer out. Unscrew the loading platform, below the loading drawer, disconnect any ground wire, and pull the platform straight up and back. Unplug the wires from the on/off switch and check it for continuity. A continuity tester should indicate continuity when the switch is in the on position, and no continuity in the off position. Replace the switch with an identical part if it is faulty.

With the power cord unplugged and the top panel off, check the power fuse. Remove the fuse with a fuse puller and touch the ends of the fuse with the probes of a continuity tester. If the tester indicates no continuity, replace it with an identical part.

If the display lights are on but there is no sound, check to see that the CD player is correctly connected to the receiver, and that all controls are set properly. Make sure that the receiver works with other sources, such as the radio or tape player.

If the problem is with the CD player, open the loading drawer and unplug the set. Remove the top panel and carefully lift the flapper that holds the disc on the platter when the loading drawer is in. The objective lens, the lens that focuses the laser beam on the spinning disc, is below the flapper, pointing up. Remove any dust from the lens with compressed air, and clean the lens with a foam swab moistened with lens cleaner available from a camera dealer. Dry the lens with a clean, dry swab.

Next, inspect the drive belts to see that they are operating properly. Open the loading drawer, unplug the CD player, and remove the top panel. Unscrew the loading-drawer guard and pull the loading drawer out through the front panel. If necessary, unscrew and remove the loading platform to reach any belts on the underside of the platform. Examine the belts for wear or damage, replacing any if necessary. Clean the belts using rubber cleaning compound and foam swabs, drying the belts with a clean swab. Avoid touching the belts with your fingers. If the CD player still does not work, take it in for professional service.

If the sound from the CD player is distorted, first check the sound from other sources, such as the radio or tape player. If this sound is also distorted, the problem is with the receiver or speaker. If the distortion occurs only with the CD player, remove the CD, clean it, and try it again.

If the CD player produces distortion with several different CDs, clean the objective lens as discussed above. Distortion can also be caused by loose or defective belts. See the discussion above regarding inspecting and cleaning drive belts.

If the CD starts to play and then stops, the causes may be any of those just mentioned, including a dirty or damaged compact disc, a dirty objective lens, or loose or damaged drive belts.

If the loading drawer does not open or close properly, check the drive belts and the on/off switch. Also check the loading motor switch, which is located on the loading platform near the gears. Check to see that the switch and its wires are not damaged. Touch a probe of a continuity tester to a wire terminal on the switch and the other probe to each switch wire terminal on the circuit board. The tester should indicate continuity only once. Repeat the test for each switch wire. Replace the switch if it is faulty.

TURNTABLES

A turntable performs two distinct functions in playing a record. Mechanically, the turntable spins the record at the correct speed and allows the stylus (needle) at the end of the tone arm to track through the grooves of the record. Electronically, the turntable transmits the electrical signals produced by the cartridge to the receiver. The stylus is mounted in the cartridge, and the cartridge converts the vibrations of the stylus into electrical signals.

If the turntable platter is spinning and the stylus is tracking the record grooves, but there is no sound, first check to see that the receiver is working properly with other sources, such as the radio or tape player. Next, see that the turntable is properly connected to the receiver, and that the controls are set correctly.

Check the instructions that came with your turntable to see if the headshell, the end of the tone arm that holds the cartridge, can be removed. If possible, remove the headshell and check the wire connections from the cartridge to the headshell. If the headshell cannot be removed, inspect these wires in place. With the headshell off, turn on power to the turntable and turn on the receiver. Turn the receiver selector switch to the phono setting and turn the volume to a low setting. There are four terminals at the end of the tone arm where the headshell was removed. Touch the tip of a very small screwdriver to each terminal. Two of these terminals should produce a humming noise through the speakers when touched with the screwdriver, and the other two should not. If more or less than two terminals produce a hum, the tone-arm wiring is faulty, and the tone arm should be repaired by a professional or replaced.

If the turntable will not spin, first check to see that it has power. With the turntable unplugged, locate the terminals for the power cord and disconnect one of the wires. Touch one probe of a continuity tester to one prong of the power-cord plug and the other probe to each wire of the other end of the power cord. The tester should indicate continuity for one wire and not for the other. Repeat the test for the other prong of the power-cord plug. If the power cord fails any of these tests, it should be replaced.

If there is still no power, test the on/off switch to see if it is functioning properly. Remove the top or bottom panel to gain access to the on/off switch terminals. With the switch in the off position, touch the probes of a continuity tester to the terminal. The tester should indicate no continuity. Turn the switch to the on position and repeat the test. The tester should now indicate continuity. If the switch fails either test, it is faulty and should be replaced.

Next, check the drive belt to see if it is loose or broken. Unplug the turntable and lock the tone arm in position. Remove the rubber record mat from the top of the platter. Find the drive belt through the hole in the platter and pull it away from the pulley. Lift the platter off the turntable and remove the belt. Examine the belt for wear or damage, replacing it if necessary.

To install the drive belt, wrap the belt around the tracing rim on the bottom of the platter. Stretch the belt toward a hole in the platter, reaching a finger through the hole from the top side of the platter and grabbing the belt. Turn the platter right side up and replace it on the turntable, slipping the drive belt over the pulley.

SPEAKERS

Speakers are relatively simple in design, consisting of an enclosure or box, two or more drivers (usually including the woofer, the tweeter, and the midrange) and a crossover network. The crossover network divides the incoming sound frequencies into the appropriate ranges, and sends each to the right driver. If there is no sound from either speaker, first check the receiver and the music source (tape player, etc.), to see that they are functioning properly and that the various components are connected correctly.

If there is sound from one speaker only, or if the sound is intermittent or distorted, the problem is usually either with a driver or with the crossover network. To check the drivers, turn off the stereo system, disconnect the speaker wires, and remove the speaker grille from the front of the speaker. Unscrew the driver from its mounting on the speaker enclosure, leaving the wires connected to the terminals on the driver.

Touch one probe of a continuity tester to a driver terminal and the other probe to the same wire's terminal on the crossover network. The crossover network is mounted on the inside of the speaker enclosure on the back panel. The tester should indicate continuity. If it does not, the wire is faulty and should be replaced. Repeat the test for the other wire.

Label the wires and disconnect them from the driver. Set a multitester to test for resistance and touch the probes to the driver terminals. The tester should indicate resistance close to the ohms rating specified by the manufacturer, either on the driver or in the literature that came with the speakers. If a driver does not register the appropriate resistance, it is faulty and should be replaced.

To test the crossover network, remove the speaker grille and the woofer. There are two wires coming in through the back of the speaker enclosure, at the terminal block where the cables from the receiver attach to the speaker. These two wires are connected to the crossover network on the back panel of the speaker enclosure. Touch one probe of a continuity tester to a terminal on the crossover network and the other probe to the same wire's terminal on the terminal block. The tester should indicate continuity. If not, the wire is faulty and should be replaced. Repeat the test on the other wire.

To test the crossover network itself, remove the wires

coming in from the terminal block and label and remove the wires from the drivers. Unscrew the crossover network from the back panel of the speaker enclosure and remove it. The crossover network will be a rectangular circuit board, and it will have a round choke coil on either end, and a series of capacitors mounted in a row between the coils.

Check each capacitor by removing one wire and pulling it away from the circuit board. Set a multitester to test resistance and touch the probes to the capacitor wires. The tester should show a sharp drop in resistance followed by an increase in ohms. Repeat the test on the other capacitors. If any capacitor fails the test, it is faulty and should be replaced with an identical part.

To test the choke coils, remove one choke-coil wire from the circuit board. Set a multitester to test resistance and touch one probe to the middle wire and the other probe in turn to each of the other wires. The tester should indicate low ohms for each test. Repeat the test for the other choke coil. If either choke coil fails the test, it is faulty and should be replaced with an identical part.

Lack of a particular range of sound from a speaker, whether bass, midrange, or treble, indicates either a faulty driver or a faulty crossover network. Test the appropriate components as discussed above.

COMPUTERS

A personal computer, like a stereo, is actually several independent components interconnected into a system. Many of these components are external to the main unit, while others are inside the case. The major unit in a computer system, what most people think of as the computer, is sometimes referred to as the central processing unit, or CPU. Some people in the industry prefer to reserve the CPU name for the actual processing chip. The keyboard and the monitor are connected to the computer by cables, as are a printer and sometimes a mouse. The computer or main unit contains the motherboard or main circuit board, as well as such internal peripherals as floppy drives, a hard drive, a modem, a video graphics card, and other options.

If the system does not appear to be working at all, make sure that both the computer and the monitor have power and are turned on. The computer itself will generally have one or more indicator lights on the front panel. If the computer's main power switch is on and these indicator lights are not lit, the unit is not getting any power. Most computers have removable power cords, so check to see that the cord is firmly plugged into both the electrical outlet and the proper socket on the back panel of the computer. Check the power cord with a continuity tester, touching one probe of the tester to a prong on the power-cord plug and the other probe to each of the terminals on the other end of the power cord. The tester should indicate continuity for one and only one terminal. Repeat the test for the other prongs of the power-cord plug. If the power cord fails any of these tests, it is faulty and should be replaced.

If the indicator lights on the front panel are still not on, and if the cooling fan inside the cabinet is not running, have the power supply inspected by a professional.

If the computer appears to be running but the screen is blank, make sure that the monitor is plugged in and that there is power to the unit. Most monitors have an indicator light on the front. If there is such a light and it is not lit, the monitor is not getting power. Monitor power cords are generally removable. Check to see that the cord is securely plugged into both the electrical outlet and the socket on the back of the monitor. Check the power cord by testing it with a continuity tester as described above for the computer power cord. Make sure that the monitor cable is properly connected to both the monitor and to the computer.

To check the fuse inside the monitor, unplug the monitor and let it stand for 24 hours to allow the cathode ray tube to discharge any built-up voltage. Loosen any retaining screws and remove the back panel. Back-panel screws may be hidden under pop-out tabs. Remove the fuse with a fuse puller and test it with a continuity tester. If the tester indicates no continuity, replace the fuse with an identical part.

If the keyboard does not work at all or works intermittently, check to see that the keyboard cable is properly connected to the computer. With the keyboard unplugged from the computer, unscrew the keyboard bottom panel and lift off the top panel. Find the terminals where the keyboard cable is wired to the circuit board. Touch one probe of a continuity tester to one prong or connector pin of the keyboard plug, and the other probe to each wire terminal on the circuit board. The tester should indicate continuity for one and only one terminal. Repeat the test for each pin in the keyboard plug. If the cable fails any of these tests, it is faulty and should be replaced.

If individual keys are not working properly, unplug the keyboard and pull off the key cap on the faulty key. The key may have to be pried up with a small screwdriver. If the key-switch assembly under the key cap can be removed, remove it and clean the electrical contact under the assembly with a foam swab dipped in denatured alcohol. If it cannot be removed, spray electronic contact cleaner on the assembly and push the switch up and down to work in the cleaner.

If the printer does not work, check to see that it has power. The printer will have some indicator lights on the top or front panels. If these are not lit, there is no power to the unit. Make sure that the power cord is securely connected to the outlet and to the socket on the back of the printer. If there is power to the electrical outlet and the printer indicator lights are still not lit, test the printer power cord with a continuity tester as discussed above for the computer power cord.

Locate the printer power fuse, checking the owner's manual for access. Remove the fuse with a fuse puller and test it with a continuity tester. If the fuse shows no continuity, replace it with an identical part.

Test the printer on/off switch by removing the necessary panels to access the switch terminals behind the on/off control. Remove the circuit board and disconnect the wires. There will be four contact points, two each in separate circuit paths. Touch the probes of a continuity tester to the two contact points in the same circuit path with the switch in the on position. The tester should indicate continuity. Repeat the test with the switch in the off position. There should now be no continuity indicated. Repeat both tests with the other set of contact points. If the switch fails any of these tests, it is faulty and should be replaced.

If the printer seems to be operating properly but the print is faint or blurred, replace the printing ribbon cartridge. If the printer continues to print poorly, clean the carriage-transport assembly. This is the mechanism that moves the print head back and forth across the paper. With the printer unplugged, remove the access cover. Clean the transport belt with a clean cloth moistened with rubber-cleaning compound. Clean the metal guide rail with a different clean cloth moistened with denatured alcohol. Lubricate the guide rail with light machine oil on a clean cloth, taking care not to get any oil on any other parts of the printer.

With the printer top panel removed, clean the gears with a foam swab moistened with denatured alcohol. Lubricate the gears with white grease, applied with a toothpick. Wipe off any excess grease with a clean foam swab. Inspect the gears for damage, replacing any that are worn or broken.

If the paper is not transported smoothly through the printer, check the instructions in the owner's manual to make sure that the paper is loaded correctly into the machine. Check the paper path to see that the paper is straight and that it is not binding. If the paper still will not feed smoothly, clean the transport mechanism. Unscrew and remove the platen plate (the platen is the large black main roller behind the paper). Clean the platen with a clean, lint-free cloth moistened with rubber-cleaning compound, rotating the platen as necessary to reach the entire surface. Clean the platen plate with a clean cloth moistened with denatured alcohol. Clean the gears at the ends of the platen with a foam swab moistened with denatured alcohol. Lubricate the gears with white grease applied with a toothpick.

CHAPTER
7
. . . .

Furniture Repairs

Many furniture repair jobs are relatively simple and require no specific experience or special tools. In addition to the usual collection of tools found in an average household, furniture repairs may require a rubber mallet, a set of wood chisels, glue, and clamps. More specialized tools can include a backsaw and miter box, wood planes, and hand power tools such as a drill, a saber saw, an orbital sander, or even a router. Serious hobbyists will eventually want major woodworking tools such as a table saw or a lathe. But these tools are not necessary for everyday household repairs. Repairs to wooden tables and chairs often involve no more than refastening or strengthening loose joints, using screws, brackets, or glue. Clamps aid in holding pieces together while fastening or gluing.

WOODEN CHAIRS

Simple wooden chairs become wobbly over time as the joints loosen with everyday use. Loose joints should be fixed as soon as possible. Letting the problem go will eventually lead to other joints loosening, followed by actual damage to joints, legs, or other parts.

There are two basic types of wooden chairs. The platform chair is based on a solid wooden seat, with the back and the legs mounted on the seat piece. The back consists of a top rail and a number of upright rods, called stiles. The stiles fit into holes in the top rail and in the seat, and form the back of the chair. The legs fit into holes in the bottom of the seat, and are connected by footrails that support and stabilize the chair.

The frame chair has a single-piece back assembly that forms the back and rear legs. A seat frame connects the back unit and the front legs, and footrails also connect the legs and help stabilize the chair. The frame may be braced by corner blocks that strengthen the frame, and allow the seat to rest on the blocks inside the frame. The seat is a flat piece that is mounted on the frame or rests on the corner blocks.

When repairing a platform chair, it may be best to disassemble the entire chair back rather than try to fix a single stile. Similarly, a loose leg may best be fixed by disassembling the entire leg assembly and reassembling the legs and footrails. Mark the legs and footrails with masking tape so that you put them back in the same positions.

Begin by pulling the loose joint apart. If the joint is very loose but will not separate, look for a nail or screw holding the parts together. It is best to separate the joint completely and to remove the old, dried glue from both parts. Disassemble the chair as completely as necessary to eliminate loose joints. Scrape dried glue off the dowel ends of the various pieces and out of the holes that these pieces fit into.

If a dowel has shrunk and no longer fits snuggly into its hole, put glue on it and wrap it with thread, or wrap it with glue-soaked cheesecloth. To enlarge a larger dowel, place the part in a vise, wrapping it with a cloth to protect the finish. With a fine saw, cut a slot down the center of the dowel. Cut a small hardwood wedge a little wider and longer than the slot and tap it into the slot with a rubber mallet. Saw the wedge flush and sand it smooth. A good all-purpose white glue works fine for repairing furniture, but carpenter's glue (yellow glue) specifically designed for wood is better.

Reglue the joints and assemble the parts, tapping them together with a rubber mallet if necessary. Wipe off any excess glue with a clean cloth. If you are reassembling the legs of a chair, place the chair on a level surface with a heavy weight on the seat to ensure that the legs are even. If possible, clamp reglued parts for 24 hours. If you don't have enough clamps for the job, leave the clamp on for 4 hours, and don't touch or move the chair for another 20 hours after removing the clamp.

To fix the back on a frame chair, remove the entire back from the chair and reglue and replace it. Remove the back corner blocks and work the joints free, tapping with a rubber mallet if necessary. Scrape old, dried glue from dowels and holes, and check to see that the dowels fit the holes fairly snugly. If not, build up the dowels with glue and cheese-cloth, or use a wedge as discussed above if the fit is very loose.

Spread a thin layer of glue on all joined surfaces and fit the pieces back together. Tap the pieces into place with a rubber mallet if necessary. Screw the corner blocks back into place and clamp the chair with pipe clamps or web clamps. Wipe off any excess glue with a clean cloth and allow the glue to dry for 24 hours.

To reglue the front legs of a frame chair, follow the same basic steps discussed above. Remove the front corner blocks and pull off the front legs. Clean off the old glue, reglue, reassemble, clamp, and let dry.

If a chair wobbles but none of the joints appears to be loose, you may be able to level the chair without taking it apart. First, check to see if there are missing glides on the bottoms of any of the legs. Replace them if necessary and see if the chair still wobbles. Next, place the chair on a level surface and rock it. The two legs that the chair rocks on are the longer legs. The chair can be leveled by sanding down the longer legs, by placing washers under the glides of the shorter legs, or by some combination of the two.

UPHOLSTERED FURNITURE

Upholstered furniture consists of four basic components: a frame, a system of springs, padding, and the covering fabric. The frame is usually wood, although some upholstered furniture is made with metal frames. Maintenance of upholstered furniture includes regular vacuuming and turning the cushions for more even wear. Clean up spills or stains immediately. Consider using a spray-on fabric protector to guard against dirt and spills.

The springs used in upholstered furniture are either coil springs or zigzag springs. A zigzag spring is a piece of strong steel wire bent in a series of U-shaped bends. The ends of the spring are attached to the frame of the furniture, usually running front to back. Coil springs are either conical, wider at the top than at the bottom, or hourglass-shaped. Conical coil springs are usually attached to a system of metal crossbars that are in turn attached to the frame of the chair or sofa. Hourglass springs are attached directly to the burlap under the seat, and are held in place by webbing.

If a chair or sofa is wobbly, check to seek if the frame is loose. If this is the cause, the frame will have to be repaired and the piece reupholstered. This is a difficult and expensive job best left to a professional. If the frame is not loose, the wobbling should be fairly easily corrected. Place the chair on a level surface and rock it to find the two legs that the chair rests on while wobbling. These two legs are longer than one or both of the other two legs. If the chair legs are missing one or more glides, replace the glides and see if the chair is still wobbly. If it is, remove the glides from the longer legs and sand the legs down. Alternatively, or at the same time, place washers under the glides on the shorter legs. Experiment with different combinations of these corrective measures until the chair stops wobbling.

If the seat is lumpy or sagging, first check the stuffing in the seat cushion to see if it has become packed down. If it has, the stuffing should be replaced. Measure the cushion and buy a piece of polyurethane or latex foam to fit. Remove the stuffing, either by unzipping the cushion cover or by finding the hand-stitched seam on the cushion and cutting it open.

Trace the outline of the top panel of the cushion cover on the replacement foam, adding about three eighths of an inch all the way around. The foam can be cut with an electric carving knife, or with a large knife with a serrated blade. Cut only on the upstroke, rather than trying to saw through the foam. When buying the foam, purchase enough polyester batting to wrap the foam. The batting will protect the foam and keep it from getting lumpy. Wrap the batting around the cut piece of foam and hand-sew the ends together. Slowly and carefully work the covered foam back into the cushion cover.

If the cushion stuffing is in good shape, the sagging is probably caused by a problem with the springs. Turn the chair or sofa upside down and remove the tacks holding the dustcover to the bottom of the frame. If your chair has coil springs held in place by webbing, the webbing may have stretched or torn. Reinforcing or replacing old webbing requires some very specialized tools: a webbing stretcher and several upholstery skewers. Unless you know someone who has these tools, webbing work is best left to a professional.

If your chair has conical coil springs, you will see that the springs are held in place by rows of twine tied to the springs and tacked to the frame of the chair. If some springs have shifted because of broken twine, cut away the twine and remove its tacks from the frame of the chair. Use replacement twine at least as heavy as the original, and cut a piece about 1½ times the width of the frame. Drive a tack partially into the frame close to where you just removed the old tacks. Loop one end of the twine around the tack and finish driving the tack into the wood. Start another tack right next to the first and loop the twine around it in the opposite direction. Then drive in the second tack.

Loop the twine around the closest part of the nearest coil spring and pull it tight. Run the twine under the spring and loop it around the coil opposite the first loop. Pull the twine tight and repeat on the next coil. When you get to the other side of the frame, attach the twine to the frame with two tacks as above. If any other twine is worn or frayed, replace it in the same way.

If the chair has zigzag springs, the springs are attached to the frame with metal clips. The seat will sag if a clip breaks or if a spring works its way out of its clip. If a clip is broken, buy a replacement part at an upholstery supply store. Do not try to put the replacement clip in the same place as the original. The new clip should be mounted on the inside of the frame, as close to the old clip as possible. Nail the clip to the frame and stretch the spring and slide the end into the new clip. Use pliers, channel locks, or vise grips to aid in stretching the spring into place.

A disconnected spring may break the twine holding it in place. If so, cut away the old twine and cut a new piece about 1½ times the width of the frame. Attach one end of the twine to the frame with two tacks, as discussed above. Stretch the twine tightly to the first spring and tie it around the closest loop of "U" in the spring. Then tie the twine around the spring loop next to, and opposite, the first loop. Continue tying the twine to each spring this way and secure the end on the other side of the frame with two tacks.

TABLES

There are two basic designs used in the construction of larger, sturdy tables. The pedestal table has a central column or stem, with the legs attached to the bottom. At the top of the stem is a support system, upon which rests the tabletop. Most other tables are some variation on a basic design of four legs attached to part of a frame, the sides of which are called the apron. The top then sits on and is attached to the apron. Smaller tables are often simply four legs attached directly to a tabletop.

If the table is wobbly, the cause may be loose joints or simply uneven legs. If the joints appear to be solid, place the table on a level surface and rock it. Notice which two legs the table rocks on. These are the longer legs. Check to see if the table legs have missing glides. Replace any missing glides and see if the table still wobbles. If so, remove the glides from the longer legs and sand the ends of the legs. An alternative or additional corrective measure is to remove the glides from the shorter legs and put washers under the glides. Experiment with small changes with these methods until you get the table level.

If the legs are loose, check to see if the legs are fastened with screws or bolts or even wing nuts. Tighten any fasteners and check to see if the table is still wobbly. The tabletop may be fastened to the apron with such fasteners also. Check to see that these are all tight.

If a joint is loose, remove the tabletop, check for and loosen any fasteners around the joint, and try to pull the joint apart by hand. The typical construction method here is a tenon on the end of the apron piece glued into a mortise in the top of the table leg. Scrape the old dried glue from the tenon and the mortise. See if the tenon fits fairly tightly in the mortise. If it does not, build up the tenon by wrapping it with glue-soaked strips of cheesecloth. Apply glue to the matching surfaces and put the parts together, tapping them with a rubber mallet if necessary. Turn the table upright on a level surface and clamp the joint with a pipe clamp. Allow the glue to dry for 24 hours.

Legs on a pedestal table are usually attached to the central stem with dowels. If a leg is loose, slowly work it loose from the stem. Try to pull the leg straight out from the stem so as to avoid damage to the dowels. Scrape off any dried glue and build up the dowels if necessary with glue and either tread or cheesecloth.

Spread glue on the matching surfaces and tap the legs back into place. Clamp the leg in place with a large clamp, wipe off any excess glue, and let the glue dry for 24 hours.

Extension tables are usually a variation on the apron-table design, with a two-piece top that pulls apart to allow an extension leaf to be added. Some extension tables are of the pedestal design, with the extension mechanism mounted on top of the pedestal.

The principal problem with extension tables is a sticking extension mechanism. Extension mechanisms consist of either wooden runners or tracks and sprockets. For wooden runners, extend the mechanism as far as possible and use a knife or similar tool to scrape any debris from the runners. Remove any wax or grease buildup with a clean cloth soaked in mineral spirits. Lubricate the runners by rubbing the parts with a candle or a block of paraffin.

Sprocket mechanisms have tracks with metal teeth sliding along a central gear or sprocket. Check to see that the sprocket is fastened securely, tightening the central screw if necessary. If the screw hole has enlarged so that the sprocket cannot be tightened, remove the screw and fill the hole with a few drops of glue and several toothpicks. Clean the sprocket and the tracks with a spray silicone lubricant and an old toothbrush.

BEDS

Many beds today consist of a mattress and a box spring resting on a metal frame. If there is a headboard, it is generally bolted onto the frame, and is not part of the actual structure of the bed. But there are beds, both new and old, that are made of wood.

A bed usually consists of a headboard, a footboard, side rails that join the headboard and footboard, and slats that rest on the ledges of the side rails and support the mattress and box spring. The side rails are usually connected to the headboard and footboard with knock-down fasteners so that the bed can be quickly and easily disassembled for movement. This fastener typically consists of a hook on the side rail and a receiving slot in the headboard and footboard.

If the bed wobbles, first check the fasteners to see if any are loose. Tighten all screws or bolts holding the fasteners. Check the side rails for cracks, particularly where knock-down fasteners are mounted in the end of the rails. If the side rail is cracked, remove the fastener and glue and clamp the crack. Cut a block of hardwood to fit in the mortice left in the end of the side rail by the removal of the fastener. Glue the block in the mortise and clamp it. Allow the glue to dry, and sand the block flush with the end of the side rail. Buy a surface-mounted knock-down hook and plate fastener and mount the hook on the side rail and the plate on the bedpost.

To install the new hook fasteners on the side rail, place the side rail flat on a table or workbench and position the new fastener on the end of the side rail with the hooks flush with the edge of the rail. Drill screw holes to match the mounting holes in the fastener and screw the fastener to the rail.

Place the fastener plate on the hook fastener and hold the side rail in place on the bed, making sure that the rail is level and parallel to the other rail. Mark the bedpost from the holes in the fastener plate. Drill screw holes in the bedpost and mount the fastener plate.

If the mattress sags to one side, check the bed slats to see if any are broken or warped. Replace any slats if necessary. Next, check the side-rail ledges, the strips of wood on the inside of the side rail that holds the slats. If a ledge is loose, tighten the screws that hold it in place. If it is warped or broken, it will have to be replaced.

Place the side rail on a flat work surface, padding it to prevent damage to the finish. Clamp the side rail to hold it steady. Trace the outline of the ledge on the side rail with a pencil and remove the ledge. The ledge will usually be held in place by screws and glue. Remove the screws and pry the ledge up with a small pry bar or a screwdriver. Buy a replacement piece of hardwood of the same dimensions as the original ledge. Cut to length, spread glue on the matching surfaces, and position the new ledge on the side rail. Clamp the pieces together, drill screw holes, and attach the new ledge to the side rail with screws.

DRAWERS

Dresser drawers can warp, sag, or stick over time. If the drawer sticks, remove the drawer and rub a candle or paraffin on the runners (rails on the bottom of the drawer) and guides (the groove that the drawer runner slides in). Check the outside of the drawer and the inside of the dresser for protruding nails or screws that might be catching. Check the bottom runners of the drawers to see if they are worn unevenly. Sand the runners, drive thumbtacks into the bottom of the drawer runners, or mount glides on the drawer guides.

Check the drawer bottom to see if it sags. If it does, remove the bottom and turn it over and remount it, or replace it. Check the drawer joints to see if they are loose. If so, reglue the joint and clamp it until dry.

If more than one drawer sticks, the cabinet may be warped or the floor may be uneven. Check to see if the dresser is level. If not, move it to a level area and see if the drawers stick. If the cabinet itself is badly warped, it will probably have to be rebuilt by a professional.

Loose drawer handles can usually be fixed simply by tightening the screws on the inside of the drawer. If the screw hole has been enlarged, try a slightly larger screw if the handle appears to be large enough that the larger screw will not crack it. Otherwise, pack the enlarged screw hole with glue and toothpicks and replace the old screw.

DOORS

Cabinet doors wear with time and use. Hinges loosen, catches break, and doors warp. There are two basic types of furniture doors: one is lipped and butts up against the door frame, and the other fits flush with the face of the cabinet.

If the door won't close completely or if it hangs unevenly, check to see if the hinges are loose. Tighten the hinge screws if possible. If the screw holes have become enlarged, pack the holes with glue and toothpicks and replace the original screws. If the hinges are tight but there is still a gap in the door, the hinges will have to be shimmed. If the edge of the door opposite the hinges is lower than it should be, remove the bottom hinge, place a shim of thin cardboard behind the hinge, and remount the hinge. If the door is still too low, use a thicker shim. If the door is too high on the edge opposite the hinges, shim the top hinge.

For further adjustment to the door, after shimming one hinge, deepen the mortise of the other hinge. Remove the hinge, outline the area to be deepened with a utility knife, and remove a thin layer of wood with a wood chisel.

If the cabinet frame is twisted or if the door itself is warped, the same process of shimming a hinge or deepening a mortise will correct a minor problem. If the problem is serious, the cabinet may have to be rebuilt by a professional.

If a door will not stay closed, check to seek that the door catch is working properly. Replace a door catch if necessary. If the door works okay, the mortises may be too deep, and should be shimmed as discussed above.

CHAPTER

8

. . . .

Heating and Air-conditioning

Many common problems involving your home heating and air-conditioning systems can be fixed relatively easily, using basic tools that you should already have in your tool kit. As with any repair of power equipment, turn off the power (and if necessary the gas) before beginning work on the heating or cooling system. It is a good idea to know ahead of time where your main service panel is (the box, often in the basement or garage, sometimes on the outside of the house, containing the circuit breakers), and have the individual circuits clearly labeled so that you can turn off the proper one in a hurry if necessary. You should also be aware, before needing the information, of how to turn off the gas to any appliance in your home, including the furnace.

HEATING SYSTEMS

The home heating system consists of three basic components: the furnace, the thermostat, and the heat distribution system. The furnace produces heat by burning gas, oil, or coal, or by using electricity. The furnace's heat exchanger then heats the air or water that is used by the distribution system to carry the heat to the various parts of the house.

There are two basic types of heat distribution systems: air

and water. An air distribution system uses a fan and a network of air ducts to move heated air from the furnace to each room in the house. A water distribution system pumps heated water through pipes to radiators or baseboard units, allowing the heated water to warm the room.

Finally, the thermostat is the control that allows you to determine how warm you want your house. Some homes have a single, centrally located thermostat, while others have several thermostats, each controlling an area or zone (or even an individual room) in the house. Many modern thermostats have timers, allowing automatic adjustments to the house temperature at different times of day or night.

HEATING CONTROLS

The simplest thermostat has a thermometer and a temperature setting indicator. The thermostat sends electrical signals to the heating system, turning the system on or off. Many heating-system problems are caused by faulty or improperly adjusted thermostats.

There are three different types of simple thermostats. They are the low-voltage round thermostat, the low-voltage square thermostat, and the line-voltage thermostat. Low-voltage thermostats run on power that is stepped down by a transformer from the household line voltage of 120 volts to a special 24-volt circuit used by the thermostat. Line-voltage thermostats are used with baseboard heaters and run on the same power used by the heating system, either 120 volts or 240 volts. It is particularly important when working with a line-voltage thermostat to turn off the power before attempting any repairs.

If the heating system does not operate at all, and there is no heat in the house, first check to see that there is power to the system. Check the circuit breaker to see that it has not been tripped.

The heating system will not function if the thermostat is dirty or faulty. Low-voltage thermostats can be easily cleaned. To clean the thermostat, turn off the power to the heating system and remove the thermostat cover by pulling it off of its base. The thermostat has a bimetal coil (a coil of flat spring metal) behind the dial. Clean the coil with a small soft brush. Turn the thermostat dial back and forth to help dislodge any dirt while brushing the coil.

If your thermostat is round, loosen the screws holding the body of the thermostat to the base (the component secured to the wall). Pull the body away from the base, along with the screws, which will remain attached, and set it aside.

On a round thermostat with the cover and body removed or on a rectangular thermostat with the cover removed, you will now have access to the control lever. This is the small lever that is moved to turn the heating system on or off. Lift the lever slightly and slide a piece of clean white typing paper between the lever and the contacts under it. With the lever over each contact, slide the paper back and forth to clean the contacts. Reassemble the thermostat and try the heating system.

If the heating system still does not function, test the thermostat to see if it is faulty. Turn off the power to the heating system. For a round thermostat, remove the cover and the body. For a rectangular thermostat, unscrew the base from the wall. Using a jumper cable with an alligator clip at each end, attach the clips to the terminals marked "R" and "W." (These terminals have red and white wires attached.)

Now turn on the power to the heating system. If the furnace comes on, the thermostat is faulty and should be replaced. If the furnace does not come on, the thermostat is not faulty and the problem is elsewhere.

For a line-voltage thermostat, turn off the power to the

heating system and remove the cover of the thermostat. Loosen the screws holding the thermostat and pull it out of the mounting box in the wall. Use a voltage tester to check again that there is no power to the thermostat. Unscrew one wire cap to bare the wires. Touch a voltage-tester probe to the wires and the other probe to the metal mounting box in the wall. Repeat the test on the other wire. Touch the probes to both sets of wires. The tester should not register any voltage on any of these tests. If it does, turn off the proper circuit breaker or remove the proper fuse and repeat the voltage test.

Remove the thermostat and turn the dial slowly from the lowest setting to the highest. As the dial passes the current room temperature, you should hear a slight click. If you don't hear the click, set a multitester to RX1, turn the thermostat dial to the lowest setting, and touch a probe to each wire. The multitester should not show any continuity. Then turn the thermostat dial past the current room temperature and test again. The multitester should now indicate continuity. If the thermostat fails either test, replace it with a similar model of the same or greater amperage. If the thermostat checks out okay, reinstall it and turn on the power.

If the heating system does not turn off when it should, or if the room temperature is consistently different from the thermostat setting, the thermostat may not be level. To level a rectangular thermostat, remove the cover and place a level across the leveling posts on the top of the thermostat base. It if is not level, reposition the body by loosening the screws holding the base to the wall, moving the base until it is level, and tightening the screws.

To level a round thermostat, remove the cover and locate the alignment marks on the top and bottom of the base. Hold a plumb line (or a heavy bolt or nut tied to a piece of string) in front of the base. If both alignment marks do not line up with the plumb line, reposition the thermostat base by loosening the screws holding the base to the wall, moving the base until the alignment marks line up with the plumb line, and retightening the screws.

Electronic Thermostats: An electronic thermostat has a digital readout and is powered by standard alkaline batteries. If the furnace will not start, to service an electronic thermostat, turn off the power to the heating system and pull the body of the thermostat off of its base. The batteries will be located in the body, where there will also be a low-battery power signal or indicator. If this signal is on, replace the batteries, put the body of the thermostat back on the base, and turn on the heating system.

If the batteries are okay, connect a jumper cable with alligator clips to the "R" and "W" terminals on the base of the thermostat. (These are the terminals connected to the red and white wires coming out of the wall.) Restore power to the heating system. If the furnace now starts, the thermostat is faulty and should be replaced.

AIR DISTRIBUTION SYSTEMS

Most modern homes have an air distribution system, since the same system can be used for heat and for central air-conditioning. The heart of the system is a blower, housed in the furnace and driven by a motor. The blower draws air from the house through the return ducts and through a filter that cleans out dust particles. The air then goes into the furnace, where it is heated, and through the hot air ducts to the rooms of the house. Air-conditioning follows the same process, with the air being cooled by the air conditioner before being distributed through the air ducts to the various rooms of the house. The furnace may also have a humidifier mounted on the supply duct, the main air duct out of the furnace, which in turn feeds to all the other ducts in the system.

The filter should be inspected monthly and changed when it gets dirty. The blower should be inspected and serviced at least once a year. Check the blower for wear or damage, clean the blades, check the belt tension, and lubricate the blower motor during this annual inspection.

If the heating system will not run at all, check the circuit breaker or fuse to make sure that there is power to the system. If the system runs, but there is no airflow from the vents, inspect the blower belt to see if it is loose or broken. With the power to the furnace off, remove the access panel and inspect the belt for cracks or wear. Push down on the belt in the middle. You should be able to depress the belt about an inch. If the belt can be depressed more than an inch, it is loose and should be tightened. If it cannot be depressed an inch, it is too tight. Adjust the belt via the blower-belt adjustment bolt located below the motor. Loosen the locknut on the bolt and turn the adjustment bolt clockwise to tighten the belt, counterclockwise to loosen it. When the belt tension is correct, retighten the locknut on the adjustment bolt.

If the blower belt is cracked, worn, or brittle, it should be replaced. Remove the old belt by pushing it over the top of the motor pulley, turning the pulley counterclockwise if the belt is difficult to remove. Slip the new belt over the blower pulley, and then work it over the motor pulley, again turning the motor pulley counterclockwise if necessary. Adjust the tension on the new belt as described above.

The next item to check is the fan-and-limit control. This control consists of a fan switch and a shutoff (limit) switch. On gas furnaces, the fan-and-limit control is mounted behind the access panel against the plenum, the part of the furnace above the burner where the air is heated before being recirculated into the house. The limit control is a toggle switch or push/pull switch that is usually marked either "manual/auto" or "summer/winter." Set the switch to "manual" or "summer." If this turns the blower on, then the blower motor is okay. If not, test the fan switch.

With the power to the furnace off, pull the cover off the fan-and-limit control. There are three wires coming into the control box. The fan-switch wire is connected to the terminal to the left of the dial. The limit switch wire is connected to the terminal to the right of the dial. The third wire is connected to the common contact slot near the bottom of the control. Disconnect the fan wire from its terminal and set the switch to "manual." Touch one probe of a continuity tester to the fan contact slot and the other probe to the common contact slot at the bottom of the control base. If the tester indicates continuity, the fan switch is okay. Next, disconnect the limit switch wire on the other side of the control dial and repeat the test. If either switch fails the continuity test, it is faulty and should be replaced.

Finally, lack of airflow may be caused by a faulty blower relay. With the power off, set a multitester to the setting 50-volt range. Attach one tester probe to the "G" terminal, and the other to the "T," "V," or "C" terminal. Taking care not to touch the terminals or probe clips, have someone turn the power on and the thermostat fan switch to on. The multitester should indicate 24 volts and the blower should start. If the blower does not start, the thermostat circuit is faulty.

If the tester indicates 24 volts, turn the power off and touch the probes of a continuity tester to the "G" and "C" terminals. If there is no continuity, the relay is faulty and should be replaced. If there is continuity, check the blower motor to see if it is working properly.

If part of the house is not getting sufficient heat, check to see that heat registers are not closed or blocked. Also, see that the blower blades are clean and that the air filter is not dirty or clogged.

If the entire house is not sufficiently warm, even with the heating system running, the filter may be dirty or the blower may be running poorly. Check the blower-belt tension and adjust it if necessary. Clean the blower blades and oil the blower motor and bearings. If the house is still not warm enough, try adjusting the blower speed.

The blower speed is a function of the width of the distance between the two halves of the motor pulley. With the furnace power off, slide the blower belt off the motor pulley, turning the pulley counterclockwise if necessary to ease the removal. Loosen the setscrew on the outer half of the motor pulley with a hex-key wrench. The outer half of the pulley turns independently on the shaft to adjust the gap and therefore the speed. Turn the out pulley half clockwise to increase the blower speed and counterclockwise to decrease the speed. Align the setscrew with the flat side of the motor shaft and retighten it. Slide the blower belt back on the motor pulley, turning the pulley counterclockwise if necessary.

Excessively noisy airflow is caused by a high blower speed or by loose joints at the duct corners. If necessary, reduce the blower speed as discussed above. Air ducts are suspended by hangers from the ceiling in the basement. Check the hangers and tighten them if needed. At the same time, see if the joints are loose and tighten them if necessary.

Excessive blower noise can be caused by loose mountings or by worn blower or motor bearings. Tighten all mounting hardware holding the motor and the blower. Lubricate the motor and bearings, replacing worn bearings if necessary.

If the blower belt slips or squeaks, tighten it or replace it.

See also "Central Air" on page 164.

WATER DISTRIBUTION SYSTEMS

Few modern homes have water distribution heating systems. Most such systems in use today were originally coal-fired boilers, later converted to gas or fuel oil. In this kind of system, a burner heats water in a boiler. A circulation pump then pumps the water through a system of distribution pipes to radiators or convectors. The system continues to pump the hot or warm water even after the burner has turned off. When the temperature of the circulating water drops below the preset level, the burner turns back on to heat the water. The water temperature is controlled by an aquastat, a control that turns the burner on or off according to the temperature of the water.

If the system is not producing heat, first check to see that there is power to the heating system. Next, check the aquastat (a water distribution heating system has at least one aquastat, and may have two or three). An aquastat may be the surface mounted type, usually mounted with bracket on a pipe, or the immersion type, with a probe inserted into the boiler.

A burner aquastat turns the burner on and off as needed, while a pump aquastat turns the circulation pump on and off. A combination aquastat contains a burner aquastat and a pump aquastat in a single housing.

To test a burner aquastat, turn the thermostat high enough to get the burner to start, usually about 80 degrees. Turn the temperature adjustment screw on the aquastat to lower the setting below 100 degrees. This should turn the burner off. Wait for a short time and turn the aquastat setting back up to its original position. This should turn the burner back on.

If the burner fails to respond to either change in setting, the aquastat is faulty and should be replaced.

To test a pump aquastat, turn the setting up above 100 degrees while the circulation pump is not operating. This should cause the pump to start. Return the setting to its original position. This should cause the circulation pump to shut off. If the pump does not start and stop as it should, the aquastat is faulty and should be replaced.

If the house is too hot but the burner does not turn off, the problem is probably with the burner aquastat. Test the aquastat as discussed above and replace it if necessary.

Uneven heat through the house is usually an indication that there is air trapped in the radiators or convectors. Radiators and convectors (a modern version of the radiator) have bleed valves to let out any trapped air. Trapped air keeps the hot water from circulating effectively, and may cause knocking sounds. As a matter of routine maintenance, bleed all radiators or convectors at the beginning of each heating season. With the heating system on, start at the top of the house. Carry a small pan and an old rag to catch escaping water. Various types of bleed valves are opened by hand, with a screwdriver, or with a special radiator key. Open the valve and allow the air to escape until water begins to flow from the valve. Close the valve and go on to the next one.

Other causes of uneven heating include a faulty circulator pump or an improperly set pressure reduction valve. These problems generally require professional service.

If there is inadequate heat throughout the house, none of the radiators are hot, and the boiler water pressure is low, check the system for leaks. Tighten any leaking pipe joints, or call for professional service if necessary. Lack of heat can also be caused by rust deposits in the boiler or in the pipes.

To correct this problem, drain the boiler system and refill it, adding a rust inhibitor.

With the power to the boiler turned off, turn off the water supply to the boiler. This is done with a valve on the water-supply pipe that leads into the boiler. This pipe is usually the smallest pipe attached to the boiler. Attach a garden hose to the drain cock at the bottom of the boiler. Open the drain cock and let the system drain. This can take a long time, and will produce odors. When the water has stopped flowing from the hose, open the pressure reducing valve and open a bleed valve on a radiator on the ground floor to make sure that there is no water in the system.

Close the drain cock and remove the pressure gauge or safety valve, whichever is mounted on the boiler. Use two wrenches, one to hold the boiler fitting and the other to turn the gauge until it is loose. Insert a funnel into the exposed opening and pour in the correct amount of rust inhibitor (available at a hardware store or a heating-supply dealer). Reinstall the pressure gauge or safety valve. Close the bleed valves and slowly open the water shutoff valve. When the boiler pressure reaches five psi, bleed all the radiators or convectors, starting on the ground floor. When the boiler pressure is stable, usually around 20 psi, turn the power to the boiler back on. Allow the water to circulate for several hours and bleed the system again.

If the radiators do not warm up despite sufficient water pressure, the air expansion tank may be full of water. Allow the boiler to cool and drain the air expansion tank. Close the valve leading to the air expansion tank and connect a garden hose to the drain cock on the bottom of the tank. Open the drain valve and then open the air release valve on the side of the tank with a wrench. When all water has drained from the tank, close the air release valve and the drain cock. Partially open the shutoff valve, and leave it partially open until you can no longer hear water running. Then open the valve completely. When boiler pressure reaches 15 psi, restore power to the boiler. Allow the water to circulate for several hours, and bleed all radiators or convectors, starting on the top floor.

ELECTRIC FURNACES

An electric furnace uses electric heating elements to warm the air that is circulated through the house via an air distribution system. Because of the rising cost of electricity, particularly as compared with the cost of natural gas, electric furnaces are seldom installed in new homes any longer.

Electric furnaces are the simplest in design and maintenance, with few parts that can go wrong. The furnace does use 240 volts, so be particularly careful in working on or around an electric furnace.

If there is no heat, the first thing to check is that there is power to the furnace. Reset the circuit breaker or replace the fuse if necessary. Inspect the furnace wiring, looking for loose or worn wires.

The next step is to check the transformer. With the power to the furnace turned off, remove the front panel of the furnace cabinet, exposing the control-box cover. Unscrew the control-box cover and remove it. The transformer is mounted on the inside of the control box, wired to the fuse block below it. Locate and disconnect the wires leading from the transformer to the control terminal block, labeling them as they are disconnected. Set a multitester to the setting in the 50-volt range and attach the probes to the wires from the transformer. Taking care not to touch the wires or the furnace, restore power and check the reading on the multitester. It should read about 24 volts. If it does not, turn off the power and check the transformer windings.

Trace the wires from the transformer to the control fuse block. Pull the connectors from the fuse-block terminals. Set a multitester to RX1K and attach the tester probes to the wires from the transformer. The multitester should indicate continuity. Test the wires from the transformer to the control terminal block (discussed above) in the same way. If either set of wires does not show continuity, replace the transformer.

Test the fuses by turning off the power to the furnace and pulling the fuses from the fuse block with a fuse puller. Set a multitester to RX1 and touch a probe to each end of the fuse. If the tester indicates continuity, the fuse is good. If there is no continuity, replace the fuse with an identical model.

Lack of heat may also be caused by faulty limit controls. With the furnace power turned off, remove the front access panel and open the control-box door. On the back of the control box you will see the front panels of the heating elements. An electric furnace may have three to six such heating elements. On each element is a limit control, a safety device that turns off power to the heating element if the element overheats.

Some models have a single wire connected to each limit control. Pull the wire off the control terminal with a pair of needle-nose pliers. Set a multitester to RX1K and touch one probe to the terminal and the other probe to the bolt that attaches the limit control to the heating element. If the multitester does not indicate continuity, the limit control is faulty and should be replaced. For limit controls with two wires, remove both wires and test for continuity.

If the heat from an electric furnace is inadequate or it is intermittent, first check the furnace for loose or damaged wires. Next, check the thermostat to see if the anticipator is set correctly for an electric furnace. The thermostat's amperage label is listed in the heating-system instruction manual or on a label on the electric-furnace service panel.

Turn off the power to the furnace and remove the thermostat cover. Mounted on the body of the thermostat is an amperage scale and a setting or pointer device called the anticipator indicator. For an air distribution system, the anticipator indicator should be set at the recommended amperage setting. For a water distribution system, set the indicator at 1.4 times the recommended amperage setting.

If you have an older-model thermostat that does not have an anticipator, the thermostat should be replaced with one that does. Insufficient heat may also be caused by a faulty limit control. See the discussion above on testing these controls.

BASEBOARD HEATING

Electric baseboard heaters are independent heating devices, not connected to a central furnace. They somewhat resemble baseboard water distribution systems. The baseboard unit may have its own control knobs, or all the units may be controlled by a standard wall thermostat.

If a baseboard unit does not produce any heat, first check that there is power to the unit. Each unit is directly wired to the electrical system, usually using 240 volts. Next, test the unit's internal thermostat. With the power to the unit turned off, unscrew and remove the control-box panel. The thermostat is usually mounted on a bracket under the panel. Remove the screws and pull the thermostat and bracket out of the control box.

Remove one wire from the thermostat by pulling it off of its terminal with a pair of needle-nose pliers or by loosening the screw terminal. Turn the thermostat control knob as low as it will go, and then turn it up slowly. As the knob passes the setting for the current room temperature, there should be a click from the thermostat. If you do not hear the click, set a multitester to RX1K and attach the probes to the thermostat terminals. With the power on, turn the thermostat control knob slowly from the lowest to the highest setting. At the lower settings, the multitester should indicate no continuity. As the control knob passes the current room temperature, the tester should indicate continuity. If the thermostat fails this test, it should be replaced.

Each baseboard heating unit also has a limit control, a safety device that shuts off power to the unit if it overheats. With power to the unit turned off, remove the control-box panel to gain access to the limit control. This is mounted on the partition between the control box and the heating element. Set a multitester to RX1K and remove one wire from the limit control. Touch a tester probe to each terminal on the limit control. If the tester does not indicate continuity, the control is faulty and should be replaced.

Finally, lack of heat may indicate a faulty heating element. With the power to the baseboard heater off, remove the control-box panel and disconnect one of the wires from the thermostat to the heating element. Set a multitester to RX1K and attach a probe to the wire from the heating element. Attach the other probe to the wire on the limit control that leads to the heating element. (This wire goes through the partition between the control box and the heating element, and is connected to the far end of the heating element.) If the multitester does not indicate any continuity, the heating element is faulty and must be replaced.

To replace the heating element, turn off the power to the baseboard heater and remove the long element panel that covers most of the unit as well as the power-supply panel, which is on the opposite end of the unit from the control panel. Disconnect the wires connecting the heating element to the household power or the central thermostat. Remove any screws holding the end panels, which the heating element passes through. Slide the end panels sideways and remove them. Remove all screws holding the heating element to the back panel of the baseboard unit. Install an identical replacement part, following the steps above in reverse order.

GAS BURNERS

The gas burner is a relatively simple component of the heating system, usually used with air distribution systems. Natural gas flows into a manifold, which feeds the gas to burner tubes, where it is mixed with air. The mixture of natural gas and air then flows through burner ports, where it is ignited by a pilot light or by an electric ignitor. The resultant flame heats air, which is circulated through the house by the blower.

If there is no heat, first check to see that there is power to the unit. Check to see if the pilot light is lit. Remove the front access panel and turn the manual-control knob to off. Wait 10 to 15 minutes for any gas to dissipate. Do not attempt to relight a pilot if the odor of gas remains.

Turn the manual control knob to ''PILOT,'' depress the control knob or a separate pilot ignition button, and hold a lit match to the pilot light. Hold the knob or button down for about 30 seconds. This allows the flame to warm the thermocouple, a safety device that shuts off the gas if it is not heated by the pilot flame. If the pilot light will not stay lit, the thermocouple may be faulty.

The pilot flame must be lit to test the thermocouple. If it will not stay lit, you may have to have someone hold down the knob or button to keep the flame lit while you test the thermocouple. Detach the thermocouple tube from the combination control (the housing that holds the manual gas-control valve). Set a multitester to the DCV scale on the lowest voltage range. Clip one tester to the end of the thermocouple tube nearest the pilot and the other lead to the fitting on the other end of the tube. If the multitester shows any reading, the thermocouple is okay. If not, shut off the main gas valve and replace the thermocouple.

Lack of heat can also be caused by a faulty transformer. The transformer is accessed through the front panel. The transformer is connected by two wires to the combination control, and sits atop the larger junction box, a plain box with various wires leading into it. Disconnect the two wires leading to the combination control from their terminals on the transformer, and disconnect the ground wire on the transformer also. Set a multitester to the ACV scale, 50-volt range. Clip a multitester probe to each terminal of the transformer. Taking care to avoid touching a terminal or a tester clip, turn on the power to the burner. The multitester should indicate 12 or 24 volts.

If the transformer is okay, turn off the power and reconnect the wires. If there is no reading, turn off the power and open the junction box by unscrewing the cover. Locate the two wires leading to the transformer and inspect their connections. If the connections are loose, connect the wires and repeat the test above. If there are no loose connections, replace the transformer. There is a nut inside the junction box holding the transformer. Unscrew it, disconnect the wires leading to the transformer, replace with an identical part, and reassemble the unit.

If the transformer is okay and the pilot light is lit, but the burner will not light, you should call for professional service.

If there is a popping or exploding sound when the burner ignites, the pilot may be set too low or the pilot orifice may be dirty. To clean the pilot, turn off the gas to the burner at the main valve. Turn off electrical power to the burner also. Allow the parts to cool if necessary. Disconnect and remove the thermocouple as discussed. Hold the gas line to the combination control steady while loosening the nut that holds the pilot light gas line. Remove the bracket that holds the pilot light/thermocouple combination. Unscrew the pilot nozzle from the pilot bracket and remove it. Clean the pilot nozzle with an old toothbrush, and use a piece of soft wire to clean out the inside of the nozzle. Reverse these steps to reassemble the pilot light assembly.

The pilot flame should be blue, with a small yellow tip. The flame should contact about a half inch of the thermocouple. The pilot flame is adjusted by a screw on the combination control.

OIL BURNERS

An oil burner uses fuel or oil to heat the air or water that is distributed through the house to provide heat. Fuel oil is pumped into the system at high pressure and forced through a nozzle that turns it into a fine mist. The mist is mixed with air and ignited by a high-voltage electric ignitor.

If there is no heat, first check to see that there is fuel oil in the tank and that there is electrical power to the furnace. A stack heat sensor is a safety device that shuts off the flow of fuel oil if there is no flame at the burner. Check the sensor to make sure that it has not been tripped. Push the reset button and see if the system starts up again. If not, call for service.

Check the oil filter to see if it is dirty. With the power to the furnace off, find the oil-supply valve, which is on the oil-supply line. The valve may be anywhere along the oil-supply line, from the oil tank to the burner. Shut the oil off by turning the valve knob clockwise. Put a drain pan under the oil filter and remove the bolt holding the filter bowl lid to the bowl. Hold the filter bowl firmly to avoid bending the oil-supply line.

Hold the filter bowl while removing the retaining bolt. Twist the bowl gently if necessary to remove it from the lid. Pull the bowl straight down and empty it into the drain pan. Dump the filter out of the filter bowl and remove the gasket from the rim of the bowl. Wipe the bowl clean, inside and out, and insert a new filter cartridge. Rub oil on the new gasket and place it on the rim of the filter bowl. Place the filter bowl tightly against the lid, making sure that the gasket remains in place. Reinsert the lid bolt and tighten it.

On a single-line system, it will now be necessary to prime the pump. Set the thermostat above room temperature, turn on the flow of fuel oil, and restore power to the furnace. Once the burner is running again, find the bleeder nut on the oil pump. This is a small plug with a nipple in the center. Place a container under the bleeder nut to catch the oil, and slide a short length of plastic tubing over the nut to carry oil into the container. Use a wrench to turn the bleeder nut counterclockwise almost a full turn, until oil begins to flow through the tube. Let the oil flow until it runs smoothly, with no air bubbles.

With a double-line system, bleed the air from the filter. There is a small nut in the lid, next to the bolt that holds the lid on. With the oil-supply valve turned on, remove the bleeder nut on the lid of the filter. When the filter bowl fills with oil, replace the bleeder nut and turn on the burner.

The pump strainer can also become dirty and result in little or no heat. With the power off, close the valve on the oil-supply line. Remove the bolts holding the pump cover to the side of the pump, and remove the cover. Under the cover is a filter or strainer that can be pulled directly out of the pump. Soak it in a cleaning solvent for 15 to 20 minutes. If the strainer is bent or damaged, replace it with an identical part. If it is not damaged, clean it thoroughly with an old toothbrush, rinse it well with solvent, and replace it in the pump. Remove the old gasket from the pump, and replace it with a new one. Replace the pump cover, tighten the bolts, open the oil-supply valve, and turn on the burner. For a single-line system, prime the pump as discussed above.

CENTRAL AIR

Central air-conditioning is usually part of an air distribution system, sharing the ducts and other parts of a heating system. The air-conditioning system itself consists of the condenser unit, located outside, and the evaporator, usually mounted in the furnace plenum. The system cools liquid refrigerant in the condenser coils. This refrigerant is then pumped through lines to the evaporator in the furnace, where the furnace blower circulates warm air over the evaporator, cooling it and sending it through the house. The refrigerant absorbs heat, is pumped back outside to the condenser, and is cooled again.

Capacitor: The condenser unit has a capacitor, which stores a dangerous charge of electricity. The capacitor must be discharged before doing any work on the condenser. A capacitor discharging tool can be made from a screwdriver with an insulated handle, two small jumper cables with alligator clips, and a 20,000-ohm, two-watt resistor. Clip one end of the jumper cable to the screwdriver and the other end to one of the resistor leads. Clip one end of the second cable to the other resistor lead. Clip the free end of the second cable to an unpainted metal part on the condenser unit. Finally, touch the tip of the screwdriver to each capacitor terminal for several seconds. Check the unit to see if it has more than one capacitor. If so, repeat the process to discharge each capacitor.

Condenser: If the outdoor condenser does not turn on, first check to see that there is power to the unit. Next, see if the high-pressure switch has been tripped. This is a safety device that shuts off the condenser if the pressure in the refrigerant lines becomes too high. Turn off the power to the unit and remove the control-box cover. The cover is on the side of the condenser unit, where the refrigerant lines enter the unit. Remove the screws holding the cover in place and remove the cover. Discharge the capacitor as discussed above.

Allow several hours for the condenser to cool, and push the reset button on the high-pressure switch. Restore power and turn on the air conditioner. If the high-pressure switch cuts out again, it may be faulty. Make sure that the power is off, the capacitor discharged, and the unit cooled. Reset the switch and label the wires and disconnect one of them. Attach a continuity tester to the wires. If it indicates continuity, the switch is okay. If not, have a professional replace the switch.

The outdoor temperature sensor can also keep the condenser from running. This sensor is a small, cylindrical object mounted in the control box. With the power turned off, remove the control-box cover and discharge the capacitor. Label and disconnect the wires to the sensor. Attach a continuity tester to the sensor. The tester should indicate continuity (this test must be done at a temperature above 45 degrees). Remove the sensor and put it in the freezer for 20 minutes. Repeat the continuity test. The tester should now indicate no continuity. If the sensor fails either test, replace it with an identical part.

While the control-box cover is off and the capacitor is discharged, you can also test the capacitor to see if it is functioning properly. Label all wires and disconnect them. The capacitor will have either two or three terminals. Set a multitester to RX1K. For a two-terminal capacitor, touch the probes of the multitester to the two terminals. The needle of the tester should swing immediately to zero resistance, and then begin to move slowly to about a third to a half of the way across the scale to infinity. If the needle does not move at all or if it stays at zero, the capacitor is faulty and should be replaced.

For a three-terminal capacitor, set the multitester to the RX1K scale and place one probe of the tester on the terminal marked "C." Touch the other probe to one of the other terminals. The needle should swing toward zero resistance, and then begin to move slowly to a point between a third to a half of the way to infinity on the scale. Leaving one probe on the "C" terminal, touch the other probe to the third terminal. The meter should register as above. If the capacitor fails either test, it should be replaced.

Excessive Noise: Clanging or rattling noise may be caused by bent fan blades or by loose access panels. To check the fan blades, turn off the power to the unit and remove the fan grille on the top of the condenser unit. If any fan blades are bent, replace the fan-blade assembly. Spin the fan by hand. If it wobbles, tighten the bolts that secure the fan-blade assembly to the motor shaft. Check all access panels for loose screws and tighten them.

Excess noise may be caused by dry fan motor bearings, or by a faulty motor. With the power turned off, remove the fan grille and the control-box cover. Discharge the capacitor, and remove the fan blades by loosening the bolts that hold the blades on the motor shaft and pulling the assembly straight up and off. Follow the wires from the motor to the contactor, the central wiring block. Disconnect one of the wires and touch the probes of a continuity tester to each of the wires. The tester should indicate continuity. Next, touch one probe to the motor housing and the other probe to each wire in turn. The tester should indicate no continuity. If the motor fails any of these tests, it is faulty and should be replaced.

No Cooling: If the condenser appears to be running properly but the system is not cooling the house, first check the fan motor as discussed above. Replace the motor if it is faulty. Check the high-pressure switch, which was also discussed above. Reset the switch if it has tripped, and replace it if it is faulty.

Make sure that the condenser coils are clean and are not blocked with debris. If the system is still not cooling, have a professional check the refrigerant, adding more if necessary.

Short Cycles: If the cooling system turns on and off repeatedly, check the evaporator coils to see if they are frosted over. Turn off the power to the unit and remove the access panel on the furnace. Frost on the coils may be caused by the furnace blower not being turned on, or by a faulty blower motor. If there is frost on the coils, run the furnace blower fan with the air conditioner turned off until the coils thaw. If the coils are not frosted, the refrigerant is probably low. Have a professional inspect the system and add refrigerant if necessary.

Leaking Water: If there is water leaking inside the furnace when the air conditioner is running, the evaporator drain trap may be blocked, or the evaporator drain pan may be clogged. If the evaporator coils are top-mounted in your furnace, they may not be accessible. For bottom-mounted evaporator coils, first remove the blower motor access panel and then remove the lower access panel to get at the evaporator coils.

With the power to the unit turned off, clean the coils with a very soft brush, using a detergent-and-water solution if necessary. Check the coils for bent fins, using a special fin comb to straighten any that are bent. Clean the drain pan by wiping out as much as possible with a damp sponge. Flush out the drain pan with a garden hose or a pail of water. Pour some bleach into the pan to prevent algae formation.

The drain trap is a U-shaped dip in the drain tube from the evaporator coils. The drain tube is usually made of plastic (PVC) pipe, and the joints are often permanently glued. If the trap is glued and the unit will not drain properly, cut the tubing with a hacksaw a few inches below the joint where the drain turns down after coming out of the furnace. Flush out the trap with a garden hose, making sure that water flows freely through the tubing. Reconnect the tubing with a straight PVC fitting of the proper size, gluing the pieces with PVC solvent cement.

See also "Air Distribution Systems" on page 149.

WINDOW AIR CONDITIONERS

A window air conditioner works like a miniature central-air system, but all the parts are contained in a single unit. The window air-conditioning unit contains condenser coils, evaporator coils, a compressor, and a blower. All repairs involve removing the unit from its window or wall mounting. Unplug the air conditioner before removing it from its mounting or doing any work on the unit.

Won't run: If the air conditioner will not run at all, check to see that it has power and that the power cord is not worn or damaged. If the air conditioner quits while running, the overload protector may have shut off the unit. Turn the air conditioner controls to off, wait for the unit to cool, and turn it back on again. To test the overload protector, allow the air conditioner to cool for several hours. Unplug the power cord and set the unit on a comfortable work surface. Remove the back panel and any other housing components necessary to gain access to the internal components.

Discharge the capacitors as discussed above. On a window unit, the capacitors are usually mounted behind the dividing wall near the fan motor, or directly behind the control panel. The overload protector is in the junction box, which is mounted on the compressor. Remove the junction-box-cover retaining clip by prying it off with a screwdriver and remove the cover. The compressor motor has three wiring terminals, and the overload protector is next to or above it, and has two wiring terminals.

Disconnect the wires from their terminals and set a multitester to RX1K. Attach the tester probes to the terminals. The tester should indicate continuity. If not, the overload protector is faulty and should be replaced with an identical part.

Failure to run may also be caused by a faulty selector switch, the control that selects the level of operation of the air conditioner. With the air conditioner unplugged, remove the control panel and discharge the capacitors. Label the wires connected to the selector switch and disconnect the wires. There should be a wiring diagram on the unit near the selector switch. The wiring diagram is used to identify the pairs of terminals to be tested. As you set the switch to each position, connect a continuity tester to the two terminals indicated by the wiring diagram for that switch position. If the tester does not indicate continuity, the switch is faulty and should be replaced.

No Cooling: If the air conditioner appears to run properly but does not produce any cool air, check the selector switch and the overload protector as discussed above. Next, check the capacitors. With the unit unplugged, remove the access panels and discharge the capacitors. You will usually have to remove the brackets holding the capacitors in place and disconnect the wires attached to the capacitor terminals. For a capacitor with two terminals, set a multitester to RX1K and attach the probes to the terminals. The tester needle should swing to zero resistance immediately, and then move slowly to a spot a third to a half of the way to the infinity side of the scale. For a capacitor with three terminals, place one probe on the terminal marked ''C'' and the other probe on either of the other two terminals. The needle should react as described above. Repeat the test, leaving one probe on the ''C'' terminal and moving the other probe to the third terminal. If a capacitor fails any of these tests, it should be replaced.

The air conditioner may also fail to cool properly because of a faulty thermostat. To check the thermostat, unplug the unit and discharge the capacitors. The thermostat is mounted on the back of the control panel, and is connected to the sensor bulb. The sensor bulb is a tube mounted in front of the condenser coils, behind the front panel and next to the control panel. Disconnect the thermostat lead wires and attach the probes of a continuity tester to the terminals. With the thermostat at its highest setting, there should be no continuity. At the lowest setting, there should be continuity.

If the thermostat fails either test, it should be replaced. Pull the sensor bulb off of its bracket and remove the mounting screws holding the thermostat to the control panel. Remove the thermostat and sensor bulb and replace them with an identical replacement part.

Finally, failure to cool may indicate a faulty compressor. With the unit unplugged, remove the access panels and discharge the capacitors. Pry the retaining clip off the junction-box cover on the compressor and remove the cover. Disconnect the wires from the three terminals on the compressor motor. Think of the terminals as being terminals one, two, and three. Attach the probes of a continuity tester to terminals one and two. The tester should indicate continuity. Repeat the test for terminals one and three, and then for two and three. If any part of the terminals do not show continuity, the compressor should be replaced by a professional.

Insufficient Cooling: If the air conditioner is producing some cool air, but not enough to cool the room, there are several possible causes. First, check to see that all controls are properly set. Make sure that the grille on the front panel is clean and free of any obstructions, and make sure that the air filter behind the grille is clean.

Next, check the coils to see if they are icing up. If the fan is on low, reset it to high to prevent icing. If the coils still are still icing, the refrigerant is low or not flowing properly. These problems need to be serviced by a professional.

Excessive Noise: Excessive noise is usually caused by loose, vibrating parts. Check to see if the front panel is loose, and tighten any clips or retaining screws. Remove the front panel and see if the sensor bulb is touching the coil. If it is, secure the bulb in its bracket. Finally, check the window or wall mounting for loose screws or bolts and tighten all fasteners.

HEAT PUMPS

A heat pump can heat or cool a home by transferring heat through the use of a refrigerant. The refrigerant can move in either direction, so the heat pump can transfer heat out of a house to cool it, or it can transfer heat into the house to warm it. In warmer climates, where the temperature seldom drops below freezing, a heat pump may be able to supply all of a home's heating needs.

It is very important to maintain a heat pump properly. Once a year, clean the coils and straighten any bent fins with a specially designed fin comb. Make sure that the unit is level, and that all bearings and other moving parts are properly lubricated.

A heat pump usually has several capacitors, which store a dangerous electrical charge. Discharge all capacitors before doing any work on the inside of a heat pump. See the section above dealing with air-conditioner condensers for information on discharging a capacitor.

Pump Won't Run: Make sure that there is power to the heat pump, and that there are no loose or damaged wires. If you turn off a heat pump while it is running, always wait at least 10 minutes before trying to restart it. This avoids pressure buildup that could damage the compressor. If the unit shuts itself off while in operation, wait at least 30 minutes and press the compressor reset button. If the heat pump doesn't restart immediately, do not try to start it again. Call for professional service.

Failure to run may also be caused by the compressor contactor. With the power off, remove the top panel and the service panel. The service panel is a side panel, usually identified by an information sticker. Remove the electrical control-box cover and discharge the capacitors. Label the wires connected to the compressor contactor and disconnect the wires. Loosen the screws or bolts mounting the contactor to the control box and remove the contactor.

Inspect and clean the contact points, using a piece of sandpaper to clean the contact points. Touch the probes of a continuity tester to the coil terminals on the sides of the contactor. If the tester registers no continuity, the unit is faulty and should be replaced.

Test the capacitors as discussed above in the section on air conditioning. Replace any faulty capacitor.

No Heating/Cooling: If the heat pump runs but it doesn't heat or cool, first check to see if the outside coils are dirty or blocked. Next, check the fan to see that it is operating properly. With the power to the heat pump turned off, remove the top and service panels. Remove the electrical control-box cover and discharge the capacitors. Disconnect the wire from the fan motor to the relay box and the wire from the fan motor to the capacitor. Touch the probes of a continuity tester to the disconnected wires. If the tester indicates continuity, the motor is okay. If there is no continuity, replace the fan motor.

Failure to heat or cool may also be caused by leaking refrigerant. Have a professional inspect the heat pump and replace refrigerant if necessary. If the heat pump heats but doesn't cool, the refrigerant is probably low. Have the unit serviced by a professional.

Ice on Coils: The heat pump should defrost itself automatically. If it doesn't, make sure that the indoor thermostat is set to "automatic heat," and not just to "heat." Next, check the coils to see that the fins are not bent. Straighten out any bent fins with a specially designed fin comb.

Check the airflow sensor tube to see that it is not blocked. With the power to the heat pump turned off, remove the top panel. The airflow sensor tube is mounted on the dividing panel between the compressor and the coils.

Loosen the nut holding the tube and gently work it free from the opening in the panel. Push a flexible wire through the tube to clean out any debris. Blow into the tube to see that there are no obstructions, and reinstall the tube.

If the coils still ice up, check the defrosting system. If the auxiliary light on the indoor thermostat is constantly on and there is ice buildup on the coils, set the indoor thermostat to "cool." Let the heat pump run for at least 30 minutes and inspect the coils to see if they have been defrosted. If they have, reset the thermostat to "heat." If the coils remain iced, check the reversing valve solenoid.

Turn off the power to the heat pump and remove the top and service panels. Remove the electrical control-box cover and discharge the capacitors. The solenoid coil has one wire connected to the fan/defrost relay box and another wire screwed into the chassis. Disconnect both wires and test for continuity. If the tester indicates no continuity, replace the solenoid coil. If the solenoid is okay and the coils still ice up, call for professional service.

CHAPTER

9

· · · · · · · · · · · ·

Security

There are many design problems in the average home that can be easily solved to make the house safer and more secure. While all homes have basic locks, a little effort on your part can improve the locks and other security devices enough to make your home too much trouble for someone to break into. And while all homes must meet certain local codes for fire safety, you will no doubt want to go beyond the minimum and make your home as safe from fire as you can. These improvements are generally well within the capabilities of the home do-it-yourselfer.

FIRE SAFETY

There are two basic principles involved in fireproofing a house. The first is to do whatever you can to prevent a fire from starting. The second is to make sure that if a fire does start, it will not spread.

The first step in preventing fires is to read and follow the instructions that came with your various electrical appliances and electronic equipment. Make sure that such things as televisions and microwave ovens are properly ventilated so that they do not overheat. Check power cords regularly for wear or damage. Do not use extension cords with high-energy appliances such as steam irons. And always make sure that appliances such as irons are turned off when not in use.

Think of fire protection when building a new home, or when remodeling an old one. The materials, such as wallboard, used in construction will meet local codes for fire safety, but often you will be able to specify safer materials for relatively little additional cost.

For example, gypsum wallboard is considered a safe wall covering and meets most code specifications, but Type-X gypsum wallboard is much better at retarding the spread of flames. Fire-rated fiberboard is very safe, while ordinary fiberboard is unsuitable for residential construction.

When building or remodeling, talk to your contractor or lumber supplier for more detailed information about local building codes and available options.

It is also possible to fireproof various furnishings in your house. Do-it-yourself fireproofing involves mixing certain chemicals in water and soaking the materials in the mix or spraying the mix on the materials. (These treatments actually make the furnishings or materials fire-retardant, not fireproof.)

Drapes or curtains made of permanent-press materials can be fireproofed with a mixture of 12 ounces of diammonium phosphate and two quarts of water. Mix the ingredients together and spray them on the drapes or dip the drapes in the solution and spread flat to dry. For natural fibers such as cotton, mix seven ounces of borax and three ounces of boric acid in two quarts of water.

To fireproof a Christmas tree before bringing it into the house, mix four gallons of sodium silicate with two quarts of water and two teaspoons of liquid dish soap. Spray the tree thoroughly and allow it to dry. Spray again, making sure to spray all the branches, both from above and below.

Older houses may have some unsafe construction that has

been eliminated in modern homes by more current building codes. For example, attached garages now generally must have wallboard on the inside garage walls, rather than leaving bare framing as was done in the past. If your attached garage does not have wallboard covering the studs, consider installing it. The wallboard helps a great deal in slowing the spread of a garage fire into the house, as well as further insulating the house. If the attic or the second story of the house projects over the garage, the garage ceiling should be covered with wallboard as well.

If possible, you should be able to close off the basement from the rest of the house. This prevents a fire in the basement from spreading quickly to the upper floors. The best protection is a solid-core, flush-mounted door. If there is no door between your basement and the rest of the house, install one if possible.

Wiring: Another potential problem in older houses is improperly installed aluminum wiring. Aluminum wiring was often used in new residential construction in the late sixties and early seventies. It is safe if properly installed, but can be a fire hazard if used with the wrong wiring devices.

Aluminum wiring is easily identifiable by its silver color, in contrast with the more common copper-colored wiring. Aluminum wiring must be used only with switches, receptacles, and connectors designed for aluminum wire. Devices designed for use with aluminum wiring are stamped with the code "CO-ALR" or "CU-AL." Using aluminum wiring with switches or other devices designed for copper wire can lead to overheating and fires.

Fire Extinguishers: Fire extinguishers are rated for the type of fires that they can extinguish. A class-A fire is one that involves solids such as paper or wood. A class-B fire involves liquids, such as grease or oil. A class-C fire involves live electrical circuits.

There are three basic types of fire extinguishers, based on the material used in the extinguisher. A dry chemical extinguisher can be used on all three classes of fires. A water extinguisher should only be used on class-A fires. A carbon dioxide extinguisher can be used on class-B or -C fires. Its advantage over a dry chemical extinguisher is that it leaves no residue.

In case of fire, call the fire department immediately. Get everyone else out of the house and try to control the fire as long as it is small and localized. To use a fire extinguisher, pull the ring pin from the handle and stand at least five feet from the fire. Aim the nozzle at the base of the fire and squeeze the release handle. Swing the extinguisher stream slowly from side to side until the extinguisher is empty. Do not try to save any of the extinguisher's contents. A fire extinguisher should always be refilled immediately after any use.

A cooking fire can be controlled without a fire extinguisher if the fire is not too large. A small fire in a pan can be extinguished by sliding a lid on the pan from the side. Don't slam the lid straight down; it can scatter the flames and burning material. Baking soda can also be sprinkled on a fire to control it.

For fires involving such things as carpeting or upholstered furniture, make sure that there are no smoldering embers remaining after the fire appears to be out. Thoroughly soak the area around the fire, and remove the carpeting or furniture from the house.

Fireplace: Follow basic safety procedures in using a fireplace. Always use a fireplace screen or glass doors when using the fireplace. Glass doors are best, because they prevent any sparks from escaping into the room. At the same time, glass doors are the most energy efficient. They allow radiant heat into the room while keeping warm room air from going up the chimney.

Never use any kind of flammable liquid in an attempt to start a fire in a fireplace. Use newspapers and kindling wood, building up from smaller to larger pieces of wood as you get the fire going. Never burn garbage or waste in the fireplace, and never use treated or painted wood. Clean the fireplace regularly, and have the chimney cleaned periodically by a professional service.

Smoke Detectors: Every house should have at least one smoke detector on every floor. There are two kinds of smoke detectors: photoelectric and ionization detectors. A photoelectric smoke detector projects a beam of light onto a light-sensitive switch. When smoke particles interrupt this light beam, the alarm is triggered. An ionization smoke detector has a small chamber filled with a cloud of harmless radioactive particles that conduct electricity. The particles conduct an electric current from a terminal on one side of the chamber to a terminal on the other side. Smoke interrupts the flow of electricity across the chamber and sets off the alarm.

Photoelectric smoke detectors respond more slowly to clean-burning fires, such as those containing paper and wood. They respond more quickly to slow-burning fires, such as those that generally start in kitchens or basements. Ionization smoke detectors respond more quickly to clean-burning fires, but are more likely to sound false alarms in the case of something like cooking smoke.

Smoke detectors should be located as close to the center of the room as possible. Air along the walls, particularly in corners, circulates much more slowly than in the center of the room, and could delay any smoke reaching the smoke detector.

Test smoke detectors regularly, following the manufacturer's instructions. Keep detectors clean to prevent dust buildup, and change batteries as required.

LOCKS AND SECURITY

Any lock or security system can ultimately be defeated. But the better the lock, the more time and effort required to break into a home, and the more likely a thief will be deterred and go elsewhere.

Sliding doors are particularly difficult to lock securely. Use a length of round wood in the track of a sliding door to prevent it from being opened if the lock is jimmied. More professional lock systems are available for sliding doors, including a hinged metal bar that mounts on the door frame and fits into a socket on the door edge. Another type of sliding-door lock is a dead-bolt lock that locks the sliding and stationary panels together.

Doors on outdoor structures and storage units often require padlocks. Buy a good padlock, with a solid brass or laminated steel case and a hardened steel shackle. Make sure that the hasp and its ring, called the staple, are also made of hardened steel. Mount the hasp so that the screws or bolts are covered by the hasp when it is in the locked position.

If you are buying a house, particularly an older house, you may want to upgrade the door locks. At a minimum, you will want to change the keys for an older house. All doors should have a good dead-bolt lock. A dead bolt is relatively easy to install, requiring a drill with a hole saw. New dead-bolt kits include detailed instructions and a paper pattern or template to indicate where the proper holes should be drilled.

Windows are particularly vulnerable to break-ins. Window locks are usually not very strong, and the lock can easily be bypassed by simply breaking the glass. For ultimate protection, glass in windows or doors can be replaced with stronger material. Acrylic plastic, better known as Plexiglas, is stronger than glass, but can still be broken, such as with a hammer. A much stronger plastic is polycarbonate, usually sold under the trade name Lexan. This plastic is virtually unbreakable. The disadvantage of plastics for windows is that they scratch more easily than glass.

Plastics can be installed in most windows in place of glass, although it will be necessary to use a silicone-based glazing compound instead of an ordinary compound. Window plastics come with protective paper coverings over the plastic. You can mark right on the paper and cut the plastic with a power saw, or order the plastic ready cut for your windows.

For extra security in unsafe areas, decorative grilles can be mounted over windows. These jobs are best left to professionals, as the mounting is the weak point in the system and must be done correctly for maximum security.

CHAPTER
10
· · · · · · · · · · · · ·

Automobiles

Although modern automobiles are increasingly complex and even computerized, there are still many maintenance and repair jobs that can be done at home without specialized tools. Routine automobile maintenance at home will save money both in the short run and in the long run, as well as avoiding tying up the car at a dealer or service center for long periods of time.

TIRES

Tires should be checked regularly for proper inflation. The owner's manual for a new car will usually give a recommended range of air pressure for the tires. Within that range, a lower air pressure will give a smooth ride, while a higher pressure will give better gas mileage. If you do not have a manual or if the tires are not original equipment, the tire manufacturer will have a maximum recommended air pressure on the side of the tire.

There are three types of tire construction used on passenger cars. Bias-ply tires have layers of cords crossing one another at angles to the centerline of the tread. These cords can be made of rayon, nylon, or polyester, and are coated with rubber. Bias-belted tires are similar to bias-ply, but also have one or more protective belts of steel or fiberglass

on top of the cord plies. Radial-ply tires have the cords
running across the tire, at a right angle to the centerline.
There are also fiberglass or steel belts on top of the cord
layers for added strength and stability.

Radial tires are more durable, longer lasting, and generally safer. Because their construction, and therefore han-
dling, is so different, radials should not be mixed with other
types of tires on the same car. Bias-ply tires and bias-belted
tires can be mixed on the same car, as long as the same-type
tire is used on the same axle.

Tires should also be rotated regularly. Most new cars
today are equipped with steel-belted radials. Proper rotation
of radial tires requires keeping the tires on the same side of
the car, and exchanging the front and rear tires periodically.

Other than maintaining proper air pressure and regular
rotation, other tire maintenance must be performed by
professionals. Check your tires regularly for uneven wear
and for vibration or pulling to the side when driving.
Uneven wear can be caused by improper tire inflation or by
wheels out of alignment. Front-end wobble, particularly if it
occurs only in a narrow range of speed, is usually caused by
out of balance wheels. If the car tends to pull to one side
while driving, check the air pressure in the front tire on the
side the car tends toward. If the car pulls to one side when
the brakes are applied, check the tire pressure and look for
uneven tire wear. Pulling can also be caused by the front end
being out of alignment.

If you keep your tires properly inflated, rotate them
regularly, and keep your wheels balanced and aligned, you
will be able to get the maximum mileage from your tires.

BRAKES

Unless you are an experienced backyard mechanic, most
brake work is best left to the professional. Check your brake

fluid regularly, particularly if the brakes seem to require an excessive amount of pressure or if the brake pedal seems to have to travel more than it should.

Brake Fluid: Brake fluid is checked and added at the master cylinder, located in the engine compartment. The master cylinder is usually located on the driver's side of the car, fairly close to the firewall (the division between the engine compartment and the passenger compartment). On many cars, the master cylinder is semitransparent, and the brake-fluid level can be seen through the side of the cylinder. On such a master cylinder, there are marks on the side of the cylinder indicating the recommended maximum and minimum fluid levels.

The brake-fluid level should be between these two marks. If the level is below the "MIN" mark, add brake fluid. It is very important to use only the brake fluid specified for your car, and to avoid getting any dirt or other contaminants in the fluid. Carefully wipe any dirt or debris from the master-cylinder cap and the surrounding area before removing the cap. Brake fluid is corrosive, so be very careful not to spill any on painted surfaces, and wipe up any spills immediately.

If your brake system requires additional brake fluid regularly, you probably have a leak in the system. Inspect for leaks, or take the car to a professional for a brake inspection. Most large automobile service centers offer a free break inspection. Don't be afraid to take advantage of this service. If you think that someone is trying to sell you brake service you don't need, get another inspection from a reputable shop.

If the car pulls to one side when the brakes are applied, tire pressure may be low, a front tire may be badly worn, or the wheels may be out of alignment. Also, the brakes may be wet. If it is raining hard, and if you have just driven through standing water, wet brakes can grab and pull the car to the side. If the brakes are wet, driving slowly with light pressure on the brake pedal will help dry the brakes. If none of these things appears to be the cause of the car pulling to the side, have the brakes inspected by a professional.

Parking Brake: If your parking brake will not hold, the cable may be loose. Most cars now have disk brakes in the front and drum brakes in the rear. If you have four-wheel disk brakes, the parking brake should be adjusted by a professional. If you have drum brakes in the rear, you can adjust the parking brake yourself if you have jack stands to hold up the rear end of the car.

If the car has a pedal-type parking brake, push the pedal down about halfway. Block the front wheels and raise the rear wheels on jack stands. A metal cable runs from each rear wheel brake toward the front of the car. The two cables may meet at a single tension adjuster, or there may be a separate tension adjuster for each cable. The tension adjuster usually consists of a long, threaded rod, an adjusting nut, and a locknut.

Check to see that the rear wheels spin freely, loosen the locking nut, and turn the adjusting nut clockwise with a box wrench. Spin the rear wheels again. If they still spin freely, turn the adjusting nut until there is some resistance. Release the parking brake. The rear wheels should now spin freely again. If there are two cable tension adjusters, repeat the steps above on the second adjuster.

For a car with a lever-type parking brake, unscrew and remove the plastic console or cover around the parking-brake lever. Some of the screws may be hidden behind the ashtray or inside storage compartments. Pull the parking brake lever halfway up. Block the front wheels and raise the rear wheels on jack stands. Depending on the way the parking-brake cables are connected to the brake lever, there will be one or two adjusting nuts behind the parking-brake lever. Adjust the nut or nuts, spinning the rear wheels by hand until you feel some resistance. Release the parking-brake lever and see that the rear wheels spin freely.

AIR INTAKE AND EXHAUST SYSTEMS

Many performance problems in cars can be traced to the air intake system, particularly the air filter and two emission control valves, the positive crankcase ventilation (PCV) valve and the exhaust gas recirculation (EGR) valve. The PCV valve takes combustion chamber gases that have leaked into the crankcase and returns them to the combustion chamber for burning. The EGR diverts some of the exhaust gas back into the combustion chamber for reburning to reduce smog.

The exhaust system on a modern car has a catalytic converter connected to the exhaust-pipe line, in between the exhaust manifold and the muffler. The catalytic converter contains a catalyst that reacts chemically with such pollutants as carbon monoxide, restructuring them into less harmful chemicals such as carbon dioxide. While the muffler and much of the exhaust pipe can be repaired by the home mechanic, any work on the catalytic converter is best left to the professional.

Air Filter: The air cleaner filters incoming air, which is then mixed with gasoline and burned as fuel. The fuel mixture burned by an automobile engine is mostly air, mixed with a very fine vapor of gasoline. A dirty air filter can cause hard starting, engine sputtering, stalling, or rough running.

The air filter is contained in the air cleaner, usually a round, metal container mounted on top of the engine. On some cars with fuel injection, the air cleaner may be an oval or rectangular device, mounted behind the radiator or on a sidewall of the engine compartment. The air cleaner will generally have a large flexible air duct leading into it.

To replace the air filter, loosen the screws, clips, or wing nut holding the air cleaner cover in place and remove it. Pull out the old air filter and inspect it. If there is no damage or oil stains, and if light can be seen through the filter material, knock the filter against a hard surface to dislodge the dirt. If no light passes through the filter material, replace the filter with an identical replacement part.

PCV Valve and Filter: When inspecting or replacing the air filter, check the PCV valve and filter at the same time. On some cars, the PCV filter is designed to be cleaned and replaced. Check the owner's manual for details on the location and service of the PCV filter. For most cars, the PCV filter is located in a holder or retainer inside the air-cleaner assembly. Check the filter, and replace it if it is dirty.

The PCV valve itself is located in many different places on different cars. The PCV valve is usually attached to a hose and inserted into a grommet on the engine block. On some cars, the PCV valve may be within a hose line from the air cleaner to the engine block. To check the PCV valve, remove it and shake it. If the valve rattles, it is okay and should be reinstalled. If the PCV valve does not rattle, it should be replaced with an identical part.

COOLING SYSTEMS

The car's engine is cooled by a liquid coolant that circulates in a metal jacket around the engine. The coolant then passes through the radiator, where it is cooled by air drawn through the radiator by the fan. The coolant is then pumped back into the engine. The coolant generally consists of equal parts of water and antifreeze. The antifreeze not only keeps the coolant from freezing in cold weather, but contains chemicals to prevent rust and corrosion in the cooling system.

Even though the coolant will retain its antifreeze characteristics over time, the rust and corrosion inhibitors do break down and become ineffective. For this reason, the coolant should be drained and replaced regularly. Flushing out the engine block at the same time that the coolant is changed also helps prevent rust and corrosion. Coolant hoses and clamps should also be inspected for wear or damage. Brittle or cracked hoses should be replaced immediately. Coolant hoses will often break without any previous sign of damage. Hoses do wear out over time, and if one breaks, it is usually a good sign that all the hoses should be replaced.

Hoses: To replace a coolant hose, loosen the clamps and remove the old hose. Take the old hose with you to purchase a replacement part. The replacement hose must not only be of the same diameter, but it may also have specific curves molded into it. When removing the old hose, inspect the hose clamps to see that they are working properly. If your hose clamps are older, and particularly if they are of the wire spring type, you may want to replace them too. Worm drive clamps are stronger and easier to use.

Whenever possible, allow the hoses and the metal connections to cool before working on them. If the old hose will not slide off the metal neck, do not try to pry it off with a screwdriver or other sharp tool, as the neck can be easily bent or damaged. If the old hose cannot be twisted off the neck, use a utility knife to slit the hose and peel it back from the neck.

To install the new hose, slide the hose clamp over the hose and rub a light coat of silicone lubricant on the inside of the hose. If you do not have any silicone lubricant, use antifreeze. Slide the hose onto the neck, pushing it flush against the base. Pull the hose clamp up over the neck, leaving the clamp about a quarter inch from the end of the hose.

Draining: To drain the coolant, allow the engine to cool and remove the radiator cap. Locate the petcock (drain valve) or drain plug at the bottom of the radiator and place a bucket or large basin under it. Open the petcock or unscrew the drain plug with a wrench. Take care not to break off the petcock if it is stuck. If the petcock will not turn by hand, spray it with penetrating oil and let it stand for a time, and then try to turn it with a pair of pliers. If the petcock or drain valve is stuck, drain the radiator by removing the bottom radiator hose.

Flushing: To flush the cooling system at home, there must be a flushing "T" installed in the system. To install a flushing "T," locate the heater hoses, relatively small hoses that go through the firewall and attach to the heater core on the inside of the passenger compartment. (The firewall is the division between the engine compartment and the passenger compartment.)

The heater inlet hose runs from the engine block to the heater core. The heater outlet hose runs from the heater core to the water pump. Purchase a flushing "T" kit for your car to fit the heater inlet hose. The flushing "T" is mounted in the hose, and has a connector that allows connection of a garden hose to the cooling system.

To install the flushing "T," cut through the heater inlet hose with a utility knife. Slide a hose clamp over each section of hose and push the flushing "T" into the two open ends of hose. Slide the hose clamps up over the ends of the hose and tighten the clamps.

To flush the cooling system, remove the cap from the flushing "T" and attach a garden hose. Remove the radiator cap and insert the deflector that came with the kit into the radiator, pointed away from the engine. Start the car and turn the heater controls to high heat. Turn on the garden hose about halfway. As the engine pumps coolant through the system, the old coolant will be expelled through the deflector in the top of the radiator. When the water flow from the deflector is clear and clean, turn off the engine. Turn off the garden hose, remove it, and replace the cap on the flushing "T."

To replace the coolant in the cooling system, find the system's capacity from the owner's manual. Drain half this amount of water out of the radiator and replace it with antifreeze. If you are uncertain of the mixture of water and antifreeze in your cooling system, you can test it with a hydrometer. You can purchase an inexpensive hydrometer, or antifreeze tester, at the automotive department of a discount department store. It consists of a small glass tube with five differently colored balls in the tube, a small rubber hose on one end and a rubber bulb on the other end. Squeeze the bulb, insert the tube into the coolant in the radiator, and release the bulb to suck coolant up into the tube. The number of small colored balls that float in the coolant will translate to a freezing point for the coolant mixture. A 50/50 mixture of water and antifreeze will float all five balls, and this indicates that your coolant mixture will provide protection in all but the most arctic conditions.

Thermostat: The thermostat is a mechanical device that maintains the coolant at a constant temperature. If the car overheats, if it is slow to heat up, or if the heater does not produce any heat, the thermostat may be faulty.

The thermostat is mounted against the engine where the upper radiator hose enters the engine block. The upper radiator hose is connected to the thermostat housing, which in turn is mounted on the engine block. If the car has an electric radiator fan, disconnect the negative battery cable and the electrical wires leading to the thermostat. Drain enough coolant to get it below the level of the thermostat and loosen the thermostat housing bolts. Pull the thermostat housing off the engine block and lift the thermostat out of its place in the bottom part of the housing.

To test the thermostat, hang it and a cooking thermometer in a large pan of water. Note the temperature stamped on the thermostat and put the pan on the stove with the heat turned on. Heat the water slowly, observing the thermostat as the water temperature gets close to the temperature rating of the thermostat. The thermostat should begin to open at this point and should be fully opened when the water temperature is equal to the thermostat rating. Turn off the heat, and make sure that the thermostat closes as the water temperature drops back down. If the thermostat fails to operate properly, replace it with an identical part.

ENGINES

Regular maintenance will eliminate most engine problems, and greatly prolong the life of your car. The two most important items here are oil changes and tune-ups. Engine oil should be changed about every 3,000 miles or every three months, whichever comes first.

You can change the oil yourself at home if you have the right equipment. The only things special that you will need are a drain pan that will fit under the engine's oil pan and an oil-filter wrench. Before you start, check the owner's manual for the recommended grade of oil and the oil capacity of your engine. Purchase enough oil for your engine, as well as a new oil filter. Since the oil filter holds up to a quart of oil, changing the oil without changing the filter leaves a good deal of dirty oil in the engine.

The engine should be just warm, enough to allow the oil

to flow freely, but not too hot to touch the oil filter and other parts of the engine. Raising the car on jack stands will make the job easier, but the oil can be changed in most cars without jack stands.

Place a drain pan large enough to hold the engine's oil capacity under the oil pan and remove the drain plug. Check the drain plug to see if it has a gasket. Replace the gasket if necessary, cleaning away any old gasket material from the drain plug or the drain-plug fitting. When the oil has drained completely from the engine, clean the drain plug and its fitting and screw the plug back in place. Hand-tighten the plug and then give it an additional one-quarter-to-one-half turn with a wrench.

Slide the drain pan under the oil filter and remove the filter. This may require an oil-filter wrench, an inexpensive tool available at automotive departments or auto-supply stores. The oil filter screws directly onto a central core called the mounting stud. Wipe the mounting stud clean and see that none of the outer gasket of the old filter has stuck to the engine. Coat the gasket and inner screw threads of the new oil filter with oil and screw the filter in place on the mounting stud. Hand-tighten the new filter.

Add the required amount of fresh oil (a funnel makes this job easier), replace the filler cap, and start the engine. The oil-pressure light may come on for a moment, but it should go out right away. Check the drain plug and the oil filter for leaks. Turn off the engine and check the dipstick for the oil level. Add more oil if necessary. Dispose of the old oil properly. Use a funnel to empty the oil drain pan into one or two empty plastic gallon milk jugs. Check with your local government for recycling locations in your area. Many service stations, automobile service centers, or oil-change specialists will allow you to dump your old oil at no charge.

The engine should be given a tune-up regularly, every 6

to 12 months depending on mileage. Modern cars with electronic ignitions and fuel injection systems generally require specialized computers for tune-ups, and this job is best left to the professional.

ELECTRICAL SYSTEMS

The electrical system of the automobile actually consists of several different systems and functions. The battery stores electrical power and provides it to the starter to start the car. The alternator generates the power needed to run the car and to recharge the battery. Electric power from the alternator is also used to run necessary accessories such as headlights and windshield wipers, as well as such luxury accessories as air-conditioning and the stereo.

Battery: The heart of the automotive electrical system is the battery. More and more batteries in new cars are so-called maintenance-free batteries. These batteries are sealed, and do not have to have water added. Maintenance-free batteries usually have a sight glass on top of the battery that is part of a built-in hydrometer. If the sight glass is green, the battery is properly charged. If the sight glass is dark, the charge is low. If the sight glass is clear or yellow, the battery's electrolyte level is low, and the battery should be replaced.

Routine maintenance of a battery involves keeping the battery and its connections clean and, if the battery is not sealed, keeping the electrolyte level up. Check a nonsealed battery regularly by pulling the caps off and checking the electrolyte level in each cell. Clean the cap and the surrounding area first to make sure that no dirt or other debris gets into the battery. Check to see that the electrolyte level is up to the mark at the bottom of each hole. If the level is low, add just enough water to bring the level up to the mark. Any drinkable water is okay, but purified water is best.

Clean the battery regularly to ensure proper contacts. First disconnect the battery cables, starting with the negative cable. Loosen the clamp and pull it off the battery post. Clean the battery case with a solution of water and baking soda. Brush the solution on the case, taking care not to get any under the vent caps of a nonsealed battery. Rinse the battery with clear water, wiping off any debris on the battery or its mounting tray. Dry the battery with paper towels or an old, clean rag. Discard the rag afterward.

Clean the battery posts and clamps with a battery brush specifically designed for this chore. One end of the brush fits inside the cable clamp and the other end fits over the battery post. Scrub the clamps and posts with the brush until the metal is bright and shiny. Replace the cable clamps and tighten the bolts holding the clamps on the posts. Dielectric compound, available at auto-supply stores, can be applied to the posts and clamps to prevent corrosion.

Lights: If a light does not work, whether on the inside or the outside of the car, first check the bulb to see if it is burned out. Next, check the fuse for that circuit. The fuse box is generally located under the dash, often on the side panel next to the driver's feet. If the fuse has blown, replace it with an identical part. If a turn signal is not functioning properly, and the problem is not caused by a bulb or a fuse, the flasher may be faulty. The flasher is an electrical device that causes a turn signal or an emergency flasher to blink on and off when the switch is on. The flasher is a small plug-in device, usually located in or near the fuse panel. Pull it out and replace it with an identical part.

Alternator: The alternator generates the electrical power that runs the car and recharges the battery. The alternator is turned by a drive belt, which is driven by the engine. If the belt is loose the alternator will not generate adequate power, which may eventually lead to a dead battery. If the headlights dim when the engine slows, the battery may be weak, and the alternator belt may be loose. If the alternator warning light on the dash comes on, either the drive belt is loose or the alternator or voltage regulator is faulty.

To check the tension on the alternator drive belt, push down on the belt with your thumb in the middle of the belt. You should not be able to depress the belt more than about a half inch. To tighten the belt, loosen the alternator adjustment bolt near the top of the housing and push on the alternator with your hand. If the alternator will not move, try prying it with a long screwdriver or a short pry bar. If it will still not move, loosen the alternator pivot bolt near the base, and again press against the alternator. When the drive belt is properly adjusted, tighten the pivot bolt and the adjustment bolt.

MISCELLANEOUS

Hard Starting: Many modern cars have fuel injection. If you don't know if your car does, check the owner's manual. Never depress the gas pedal when starting a car with fuel injection. This can flood the engine, and make it impossible to start the car for hours. If a car with fuel injection will not start and you smell gas, let the car sit for as long as possible before trying to start it. A badly flooded engine may have to sit for 24 hours before it will start.

If a car without fuel injection is hard to start, try pumping the gas pedal to get the engine to catch. If the engine is flooded, hold the gas pedal to the floor without pumping the pedal and try again to start the engine.

Vapor Lock: In very hot weather, the heat can cause the gasoline in the fuel line to vaporize, blocking the flow of you may someday experience a breakdown or some other roadside emergency. Additional preparations can minimize the risk and irritation of such emergencies. The more emergency equipment that you can regularly carry in your car, the better prepared you will be for problems.

At a minimum, a car should be equipped with a first-aid kit, a flashlight, and some basic tools. A small tool kit consisting of pliers, several sizes of adjustable wrenches, and some screwdrivers, both standard and Phillips, will greatly aid in many minor repair jobs. Also keep some strong wire and some duct tape in the trunk for emergency patch jobs. A small ABC fire extinguisher in the trunk or mounted under the dash is also a very valuable emergency tool. If there appears to be a fire under the hood of the car, be very careful in opening the hood. If there are flames under the hood or near the gas tank, get away from the car immediately and call the fire department.

Flares or reflective warning signals provide good protection from other cars if you must stop on the side of the road at night, but be very careful in using flares around spilled gas or flammable roadside trash or undergrowth.

If you regularly travel long distances in winter or on back roads, more substantial survival gear is appropriate. Depending on personal needs and local conditions, you may want to include drinking water, nonperishable food, blankets, and other equipment.

fuel to the engine. The result is loss of power or even stalling. Park in a shaded spot if possible, and turn the engine off. Allow the car to cool for as long as possible, 30 minutes at the least. If water is available, pour it on the fuel pump and the fuel line and try to restart the car.

Hand-Brake Light: If the hand-brake light stays on when you start the car, even though the hand brake is off, the brake fluid is low. Check the brake fluid as discussed above, and add fluid if needed.

Frozen Door Lock: To thaw a frozen door lock, hold the key in a gloved hand and heat the key with a cigarette lighter or with matches. Quickly insert the key into the lock and gently work it from side to side. Repeat if necessary.

Windshield Washers: If the windshield washers do not work, first check to see that there is fluid in the reservoir. This is usually a semiclear plastic bottle mounted in the engine compartment close to a front wheel. On some cars, the reservoir is hidden out of sight, and the filler hole may not be obvious. Check the owner's manual for directions. Always fill the reservoir only with fluid specifically designed for windshield washers. If there is fluid in the reservoir and the washers still don't work, check to see if the washer nozzles on the hood of the car are blocked. Remove any debris and clean out the nozzle hole with a needle or a pin. If the nozzle is blocked with ice, remove as much surface ice as possible and heat a pin with a cigarette lighter or a match to remove ice from inside the nozzle.

Jump-Starts: If a car won't start because of a dead battery, it can usually be jump-started from another car using jumper cables. Check the owner's manual first to see that the car can be jump-started. With both cars turned off, attach the red jumper cable to the positive terminal of the good battery and then to the positive terminal of the dead battery. Attach the black jumper cable to the negative terminal of the good battery, and then attach the other end of the black jumper cable to a good ground on the car with the dead battery. A good ground would be an unpainted bolt on the engine block or the chassis of the car. Try to attach the cable at least a foot from the dead battery, and avoid touching any electrical equipment. Start the car with the good battery and allow it to run for a minute or two. Now start the car with the dead battery. Remove the jumper cables by reversing the steps listed above.

Garage: A well-equipped and well-organized garage makes it much easier to perform car maintenance and repairs. Tools should be handy and easy to locate. A good toolbox or a Peg-Board with an individual spot for each tool works best. The garage is a good place to mount an all-purpose (ABC) fire extinguisher, as well as a first-aid kit.

Good lighting is as important in the garage as in any work area. Proper lighting not only makes the job easier and more pleasant, it makes the working conditions much safer. A couple of fluorescent shop fixtures hung from the ceiling will give good overall light, and a work light with a protected bulb and an extension cord will provide extra light where needed. Electrical outlets in a garage, as in any outdoor location, should be ground-fault-protected to prevent accidents when working around water or even damp conditions.

It is also easier and more pleasant to work in a clean environment. Keep a large garbage can handy for trash and a push broom for general cleanup at the end of the project. A bag of cat litter will absorb most spills, even oil. Keep a bag handy, especially when changing oil. Just sprinkle it on the spill, give it a few minutes to absorb, and sweep it up.

Emergencies: No matter how well you maintain your car,